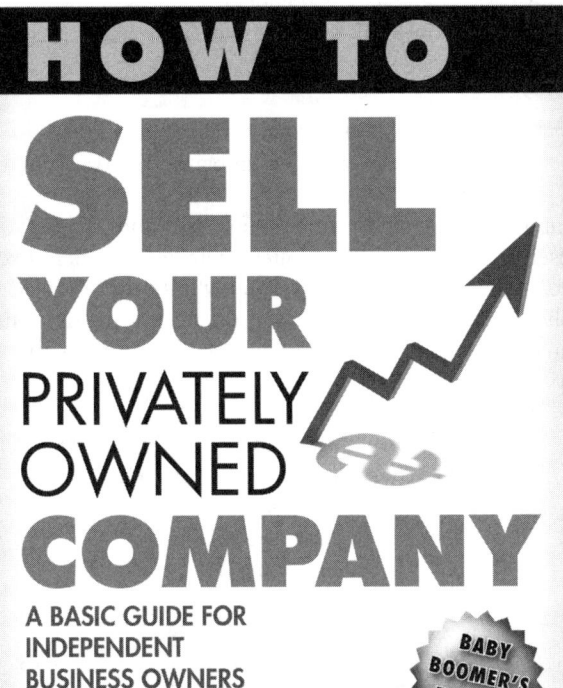

How to Sell Your Privately Owned Company
A Basic Guide for Independent Business Owners
BABY BOOMER'S EDITION
By Eric R. Voth

ISBN 978-0-9840501-4-7 – Printed Edition
WGAw Registration Number 1362531

Copyright © MMIX by ERV Productions, Inc. and Eric R. Voth. All rights reserved. Printed in the United States of America. Except as permitted under the United States Copyright Act of 1976, no part of this publication may be reproduced or distributed in any form or by any means, or stored in a database or retrieval system, without prior written permission of the publisher.

Published by ERV Productions, Inc., Eric R. Voth
19102 Polo Meadow Drive, Humble, TX 77346
Desk: 281-852-4707
E-mail: eric@ervproductions.com
Web: http://ervproductions.com/

Cover design by Denise Sedgwick
Art Director/Graphic Designer – Fort Worth, TX 76137
Desk: 817-479-8012 – Cell/Text: 832-407-4795
E-mail: Me@DeniseAtHome.net

Interior design by www.KarrieRoss.com

This publication is designed to provide accurate and authoritative information in regard to the subject matter covered. It is produced with the understanding that the publisher is not engaged in rendering legal, accounting, or other professional service. If legal advice or other expert assistance is required, the services of a competent professional person should be sought.

From a declaration of principles jointly adopted by a committee of the American Bar Association and a committee of publishers.

ACKNOWLEDGEMENTS

Rarely is the production of a creative work dependent solely upon the skills and abilities of one person. This book is no exception. The author greatly appreciates contributions of the following individuals and firms in the production of this book:

- Judith P. Christy, Clinton, Ohio – research
- Kerney Laday Jr., Dallas, Texas – contributing writer
- Cynthia Lerner, Denver, Colorado – proofreader
- David Mahmood, Dallas, Texas – contributing writer
- Scott D. Mashuda, Pittsburgh, Pennsylvania – contributing writer
- Doug Ortega, Dallas, Texas – contributing writer
- Andrew Rogerson, Sacramento, California – contributing writer
- Karrie Ross, Los Angeles, California – graphic design
- Denise C. Sedgwick, Fort Worth, Texas – graphic design
- George Sierchio, Parsippany, New Jersey – contributing writer
- David A. Wilson, Cuyahoga Falls, Ohio – editor

TABLE OF CONTENTS

Introduction 11

Overview
    This book: What's in it for you? 19

CHAPTER ONE
Making the Decision to Sell Your Business 25

    Am I bored with this business? 26
    Am I concerned about the direction of the economy
        and how it will affect my business? 26
    Is my industry changing too fast? 27
    Do I plan to retire in the near future? 27
    Are the key decision makers in my company
        moving in the right direction? 28
    Does my business offer a specialty product or
        service that a larger company wants? 29
    Do I need to sell this business to make room or to
        raise cash for my other interests? 30
    Am I faced with a personal challenge, such as an
        illness or prospective divorce? 30
    Why am I doing this? 30
    Why sell? 32
        By George Sierchio, contributing writer
    Fat, dumb and happy 34
        By Andrew Rogerson, contributing writer

CHAPTER TWO
Getting the Right Help 43

    For sale by owner? 43
    My first radio show 45
        By Scott D. Mashuda, contributing writer
    The cost of selling a business. 51
    Someone to make it legal 51
    What's a lawyer to do? 52
    Someone to make it lucrative. 53
    What's an accountant to do? 53
    Someone to make it happen 53
    What's an intermediary to do? 56
    Keeping the confidence 56
    Paying now instead of later 57
    Check them out. 58
    Your commitment 58
    Selecting the best business broker to sell your business . .59
        By Scott D. Mashuda, contributing writer

CHAPTER THREE
Putting a Price Tag on Your Business 67

    Blood, sweat, tears, and dollars 67
    What's happening outside your doors? 68
    It's about timing 68
    What goes in affects what goes out 69
    Your product or service 69
    Your management team 70
    Your customer base 70
    Your place in the industry 70
    Your industry in the place 71
    Your commitment to "just in time" 71
    Your location 71
    Your research and development efforts 71
    Your employee pension fund 72
    Your balance sheet 72

No perfect world 73
How does your business look? 73
How much is this business really worth? 74
You're too close 74
It's easy with a crystal ball 75
Capitalized Earnings Method. 75
Excess Earnings Method 76
Balance Sheet Method 77
Cost to Create Method 77
Industry Multipliers Method 77
Pricing sources 77
A common thread 77
The defense rests 79
Understanding the language 79
    By Scott D. Mashuda, contributing writer
Pricing a cash-negative company 83
    By Scott D. Mashuda, contributing writer

CHAPTER FOUR
Preparing a Plan for Selling Your Business 89

Seller with a timeline 89
    By George Sierchio, contributing writer
Would your "house" be ready to show? 91
Time to fix things up 91
Many businesses may take up to one year to sell 91
First impressions 92
What would be said about your business? 92
Make them drool 94
Appearance should not be deceiving 94
What do you need to change 95
    (regarding physical appearances)?
Documentation: Creating a Management Book 95
Employees 99
Liabilities 99
Assets 100
Contracts 101

Reputation 102
Financial Statements 102
No wonder it takes a year! 104
Creating your preliminary prospectus 104
Sales Pitch 106
Photographs/Video/PowerPoint on CD 106
Company History 106
Selling Price and Terms 107
Company External Environment 107
Employee Information 108
Asset Assessment 109
Environmental Issues 110
Generic Client List 111
Contracts and Agreements 111
Location 112
Projections 112
Supporting Financial Documentation 112
Product and Service Literature 113
Caution! 113
Summary information checklist 114
Required information 116
    By Scott D. Mashuda, contributing writer

CHAPTER FIVE
Finding the Right Buyer for Your Business 123

Whom would you pick to buy your business? 123
Selling to a competitor. 124
Customers or suppliers 125
Could employees be buyers? 125
Isn't anyone qualified to buy? 126
Investor Groups. 126
Strength in size and numbers 126
Industry Consolidators.......................127
In search of the right buyer. 128
In confidence 128

Who is the buyer for your business? 129
    By Scott D. Mashuda, contributing writer
Maximize your company's selling price. 131
    By David Mahmood, contributing writer

CHAPTER SIX
Making the Right Deal 137

What's your worry? 137
Buyers lose sleep too 138
Rest assured 138
You play the banker 139
Taking stock in the buyer's company 140
Dealing with differences 141
Call in the experts 142
Get into the buyer's head 143
A common negotiation strategy 143
Commit in writing 143
Show me the money! 144
Due diligence 145
The Agreement to Purchase 146
K.I.S.S. 146

CHAPTER SEVEN
Successfully Closing the Sale—and the Door 149

The moment of truth 149
The fastest year in history 149
What's your plan? 150
Your personal plan 150
The Wheel of Life 151
Physical Health 153
Relationships and Family Life 154
Ethical and Spiritual Concerns 154
Mental Attitude 154
Financial 155
Social Life 155

CHAPTER EIGHT
In Conclusion 159

    Go back to the beginning 159
    Why exit planning? 160
        By Kerney Laday Jr. and Doug Ortega,
        contributing writers
    You too will die. Not if, but when 162
        By David Mahmood, contributing writer
    Your worst enemy 164

CHAPTER NINE
Glossary of Terminology 167

CHAPTER TEN
Internet Resources and Words of Caution! 177

CHAPTER ELEVEN
Profiles of Contributing Writers 183

    Kerney Laday Jr., Dallas, Texas 183
    David Mahmood, Dallas, Texas 185
    Scott D. Mashuda, Pittsburgh, Pennsylvania 187
    Doug Ortega, Dallas, Texas 189
    Andrew Rogerson, Sacramento, California 191
    George Sierchio, Parsippany, New Jersey 192
    Eric R. Voth (author), Humble, Texas 194

INTRODUCTION

Like you, I have experience as an independent business owner.

During the course of my career, I have personally undertaken…

- The startup of 10 independent businesses
- The purchase of five independent businesses
- The sale of five independent companies (two of which were actually mergers)
- The startup of four franchise operations
- The loss of my investment in four independent businesses that were unsuccessful

These experiences allow me the unique perspective of being able to empathize with you as you contemplate the sale of your company. I'm familiar with the mix of feelings and emotions that sometimes accompany such thoughts. I've had them myself.

This introduction is designed to acquaint you with my background as an "in-the-trenches" business owner. Perhaps you can identify with some of my experiences.

The genesis of this book

The genesis of this book dates back to 1962, the year I graduated from high school. Three months after graduation, I began my first full-time job, a radio dispatcher for a private ambulance service in Akron, Ohio.

I became an ambulance attendant, then a driver, and was subsequently promoted to general manager of Physicians & Surgeons (P&S) Ambulance Service. In 1971, the company's founder became ill and unexpectedly died. No succession plan was in place. No heirs were interested in operating the business. A year later, my business partner – who was the assistant general manager – and I bought the company. Terms of the deal consisted of no money down, and monthly payments to the founder's widow for a period of 10 years, at a fixed rate of interest.

Under our management, the business was successful and profitable.

In 1974, we purchased a local competitor. In 1976, we expanded to Cleveland, 30 miles north of our home base, and to Canton, 20 miles south.

Seat-of-the-pants management

By 1979, our company was in a hyper-growth mode. Sales volume increased to a point where our management infrastructure was on overload. Service to our clients began to suffer. We were plagued by employee turnover and people-management problems. Supervisors lacked leadership skills. Personnel policies were poorly administered. Scheduling problems caused excessive overtime. There were inventory, supply, and purchasing problems.

We knew we needed help. We contacted the Service Corps of Retired Executives (SCORE), who referred us to a professor at the University of Akron's College of Business Administration. The professor brought in a team of four students to conduct a total case study of our company. For three months, the students poked and probed into every corner of the business. Their final report was a two-inch-thick document containing an outline of problems they uncovered, and recommendations of solutions.

It was obvious that neither my partner nor I had any formalized education or training in operating a business. We were, after all, "ambulance guys" – technicians – who had stumbled into the world of entrepreneurship and business ownership almost by accident.

The report said that both of the owners were "wearing too many hats." We were scattered in our efforts. We spent most of our time "putting out fires," instead of working to prevent them. There was no defined corporate philosophy. We practiced "management by memo." Company policies consisted of endless memos tacked to bulletin boards.

Communications inside the company were poor. Overall accountability was lacking. Neither managers nor supervisors had been trained in human relations skills. New employee orientation was inadequate. Because there was no formalized budgeting system, spending in some areas was out of control. The company did not have a focused mission that was understood by all personnel.

Making the transition from entrepreneurship to professional management

The company was passing through a critical state of growth. It was obvious that a major restructuring was in order. We needed to make a transition from an entrepreneurship to a professionally managed firm.

To accomplish this, we met with consultants and advisors, and outlined a plan of action. Various departments were created, along with an organizational chart outlining a "chain of command and accountability." Operating philosophies were put on paper and converted to company policies. A comprehensive personnel policy manual was published, along with written job descriptions for everyone.

We recruited qualified department managers, and became one of the first private ambulance companies in the country to have a full-time sales and marketing department. A director of finance was brought in to oversee accounting functions and the installation of our first computer system. Annual department budgets were created. Managers were hired for all of our outlying divisions. An administrative services department was created to handle human resource functions. We promoted employees to jobs of purchasing director and supervisor of vehicle maintenance.

Later we added a training officer to act as a liaison with our medical directors and to coordinate continuing education activities for our paramedics.

We hired full-time customer service personnel in our marketing department to monitor the care that customers received while riding in our ambulances.

During the reorganization, we recognized a need for ongoing management and supervisory training. This resulted in our personnel routinely attending classes on creative thinking, leadership, time management, goal setting, and human relations.

A committee of department managers and supervisors worked with an outside consulting firm to create a corporate mission statement and to define mission statements for each department.

In reality, we applied big business management techniques to our small, growing company... with positive results. Within a year, sales revenue and profits were up. Employee morale improved. Turnover decreased. Excessive overtime payroll expense was reduced, along with other spending. Compared to a year earlier, field operations were running smoothly.

Expanding into a new market

Experiencing these changes gave us the confidence to embark upon a bold expansion. Following the reorganization in the early 1980s, we wanted to grow, but not locally. Census figures indicated Northeast Ohio was losing its population. Like many others during that era, we looked south, toward the Sun Belt. Of the major cities there, Houston, Texas, was the fastest growing. My partner and I made a site visit to Houston to see if there were opportunities for expansion. We met with city officials and talked to owners of several local ambulance companies. After the trip, we decided that the Houston market was ripe for the startup of a high-quality private ambulance service.

We spoke with our bankers and explained our intentions. They agreed to provide the necessary financing. For the next six months, we worked to design expansion plans for Texas. A consultant was engaged to write a business plan. We selected qualified personnel from Ohio who wanted management jobs in Houston. We secured real estate, bought ambulances and equipment, and hired personnel. In January 1983, we opened the doors of P&S Ambulance Texas. After eighteen months of operation, the Houston venture reached a financial break-even point and began supporting itself.

In late 1988, we decided to expand again, this time closer to our home base in Ohio. In January 1989, we purchased a major competitor in Akron. Several months later, at a strategic planning retreat with the management team, we decided to exit the Cleveland market. In June 1989, we sold our Cleveland division to our largest competitor there.

An industry consolidates

In 1992, the private ambulance industry in the United States began a metamorphosis that rapidly transformed the pattern of ambulance company ownership. While thousands of small mom and pop ambulance services dotted the landscape from coast to coast, a few large companies began buying mid-sized medical transportation firms.

The first of these large companies was American Medical Response (AMR). It was formed in mid-1992 when venture capitalists bought and merged two East Coast and two West Coast ambulance companies. The chief officers of the original four companies stayed at their posts and became members of the AMR board of directors. AMR was the first ambulance company to "go public," putting the symbol EMT on the Big Board of the New York Stock Exchange in August 1992.

In late 1993, my partner and I were approached by American Medical Response and invited to join its family of companies. After giving the matter considerable thought, we decided to accept the offer. In February 1994, we merged our companies in Ohio and Texas with AMR.

My partner signed a two-year agreement to remain as president of the AMR subsidiaries in Akron and Houston. I signed a contract to become an independent merger and acquisition consultant for the company. My task was to approach other ambulance service owners and determine their suitability as acquisition candidates for AMR.

During this period, several other traditionally local, blue collar service-sector industries and "mom and pop Main Street businesses" were being consolidated through roll-up efforts by Wall Street investment firms.

I recognized an opportunity in this activity, and broadened my scope of merger and acquisition services beyond that of the ambulance industry. I began providing "bird dog services," matching privately owned business sellers with publicly traded company buyers in a number of different industries. Today I work in a similar capacity, matching sellers of independent companies with qualified investment bankers, merger and acquisition (M&A) intermediaries, or business brokers.

My other careers: Entrepreneurship, speaking, consulting

Concurrent with my career in the private ambulance industry, I also was involved in a number of other business ventures. I operated a direct-mail business, selling books through the mail. I opened a collection agency whose sole client was my ambulance service, owned and operated a franchised management training company, and invested in a franchised photography business specializing in portrait photography for church membership directories. As a startup, I owned and help operate a retail portrait photography studio that was subsequently sold. I owned a specialty advertising service that sold advertising space on plastic protective covers placed on telephone books. I currently own a television production company, and am an investor in a pop-culture clothing firm. I'm also an investor in a residential and commercial moving company franchise.

After my ambulance company went through its restructuring process in the early 1980s, I became thoroughly convinced that any growing business could operate more profitably – and experience fewer problems – if its owner would embrace philosophies and implement the practices of professional management techniques. What worked at my company was certainly suitable for other small businesses.

Drawing upon my personal experience in the practical application of these ideas, I developed a series of how-to seminars and lectures. They were aimed at owners of other businesses who were facing the challenge of making the transition from an entrepreneurship to a professionally managed firm. Beginning in 1980, I conducted these seminars and workshops throughout the country at annual conventions of small-business owners in a variety of industries. As a consultant, I worked one-on-one with company owners, helping them implement the strategies at their firms.

Passing it on

I'm grateful for the good fortune I enjoyed in the private ambulance business and other assorted ventures. It formed a foundation for what I do now. (I wish I knew in 1972 what I know today!) Most of my accomplishments came about as the result of hard work, long hours, lots of energy, abundant commitment, and sometimes just plain luck.

I consider this book my contribution to other independent business owners. Hopefully, the information it contains will help flatten your learning curve.

The late Dr. Ken McFarland – a professional speaker – once said, "The finest form of ministry is found in teaching others to live more abundantly by sharing the lessons of one's own experience of the past." I subscribe to Dr. McFarland's philosophy. I want to help others to know now what I have learned. I want to "pass it on," to share my knowledge with you. It's my sincere hope that the information you're about to study will prepare you for the biggest sale you'll probably ever make in your life – the sale of your privately owned company.

Eric R. Voth

OVERVIEW

This book: What's in it for you?

Did you ever find yourself in conversation with some of your colleagues, your family members, or perhaps, just yourself – when the topic of selling your business was mentioned?

Perhaps the conversation went something like this:

"I really ought to think about selling the business."

"Oh, really. Why's that?"

"Well, several things come to mind:

- I'd like to think about retiring,
- I'm worried about the economy,
- There's a lot of change going on in my industry right now,
- It's growing too fast for me – all of the details are becoming too complicated for me to handle,
- There's really no one to take over and run the place when I'm gone,
- Personally, I want to move in some other directions,
- I think I could pocket some pretty good money."

"Hmmmm."

"But I wonder if this is the right time."

"I dunno."

(PAUSE)

"But, I really ought to think about selling the place."

"I wonder what's involved in the process?"

Obviously, you can paraphrase your dialogue with the pertinent names and concerns related to your life, remembering that, for one reason or another, you made the choice to read this book.

And that's the first step – making the decision to sell. Here is a brief outline of the additional activities in which you'll be involved after making your decision.

The second step is choosing a professional business intermediary to guide you through the process.

The third step involves a complete analysis of your company to determine its value. You will need a professional valuation and an appraisal of hard assets to establish an asking price.

The fourth step is preparation of a marketing plan. This involves gathering and assembling data, and presenting it in a logical manner. A part of the marketing plan is the preparation of a confidentiality agreement. Other parts involve creating a preliminary prospectus or selling memorandum and assembling a management book containing all relevant information a prospective buyer needs to reach a decision to purchase.

The fifth step is locating qualified buyers, verifying their credentials, and verifying their financial ability to purchase your company. This step also involves showing your business by taking qualified buyers on tours of your facilities.

The sixth step is the actual negotiation of the deal with the buyer. It involves negotiating terms and conditions of the sale, and includes warranties and representations about a number of issues that are of concern to both you and to the buyer. The negotiation process leads to the preparation of a letter of intent, which is the foundation for the actual written sales contract.

The seventh and final step is the closing process, where all the papers are signed and the business actually changes hands.

If you're like most business owners, you want two things to happen during this process. First, you want most of these steps to take place under a cloak of secrecy. Second, especially if you're a hands-on manager involved in the day-to-day activities of running your company, you don't want this process to disrupt your operations. Information in this book explains how to achieve both of these goals.

HOW TO SELL YOUR PRIVATELY OWNED COMPANY is a way for you to examine many aspects of selling your business in a risk-free environment. It's designed to give you some important information you'll need to know and some answers to the questions you'll need to ask before making a commitment to actually selling your company.

In this book, you'll examine the following aspects of the selling process:

Chapter 1 – Making the Decision to Sell Your Business

Chapter 2 – Getting the Right Help

Chapter 3 – Putting a Price Tag on Your Business

Chapter 4 – Preparing a Plan for Selling Your Business

Chapter 5 – Finding the Right Buyer for Your Business

Chapter 6 – Making the Right Deal

Chapter 7 – Successfully Closing the Sale... and the Door

Chapter 8 – In Conclusion

Chapter 9 – Glossary of Terminology

Chapter 10 – Internet Resources and Words of Caution!

Chapter 11 – Profiles of Contributing Writers

CHAPTER ONE

Making the Decision to Sell Your Business

Making the Decision to Sell Your Business

A key question to ask yourself when deciding to sell your business is: WHY?

As you read in the opening dialogue, there can be a myriad of reasons for doing so based on your age, your retirement aspirations, your financial goals, or your visions of bigger, better, brighter things.

Ask yourself these questions:

- Am I bored with this business… or just plain worn out?
- Am I concerned about the direction of the economy and how it will affect my business?
- Is my industry changing too fast?
- Do I plan to retire in the near future and have no family member interested in the business?
- Are the key decision makers in my company moving in the same direction?
- Does my business offer a specialty product or service that a larger company wants?
- Do I need to sell this business to make room or raise cash for my other interests?
- Am I faced with a personal challenge, such as an illness or prospective divorce?

Am I bored with this business...or just plain worn out?

Despite the thrill of opening a business, growing and expanding it, at some point some business owners get bored, or they're just plain worn out. They have fought the battles of growing their market share, landing new customers and clients, pleasing the old ones, and buying new equipment (sometimes financed at the bank with personal guarantees and second mortgages on their homes). They've grown weary of adding personnel (and paying for fringe benefits), filing government forms, and outfoxing the IRS. Perhaps they've become totally and completely bored with running the business because now everything is so routine – and sometimes complicated. Maybe they need to do themselves – and the business – a favor. Maybe they need to sell it.

Am I concerned about the direction of the economy and how it will affect my business?

What goes up must come down. Economies, and the companies that operate within them, have always been subject to cycles. Often it is difficult to predict the intensity of a cycle and length of time between recession, recovery, growth, and decline.

In a general sense, factors that shape business cycles are many. Such factors include the volatility of investment spending, consumer confidence, technological innovation, variations in inventories, fluctuations in government spending, political motivation, monetary policies, and fluctuations in imports and exports.

Cycles also occur within specific industries and markets.

Weathering business cycles requires a long-term view that focuses on a firm's key strengths. It involves planning with greater discretion. Funding structures and long-range forecasting need to be considered. Attention to customers must be heightened. In challenging economic times, decisions based on hopes and desires, rather than an objective consideration of the facts, can devastate a business.

If these factors are causing you undue anxiety, perhaps now is the time to seriously consider the sale of your company.

Is my industry changing too fast?

If my industry is changing, do I have the fortitude, energy, and enthusiasm to change with it?

Government regulations, government policies, government reforms. Global competition. State-of-the-art technology. Big business. Consolidation of traditionally fragmented "mom and pop" industries by larger, publicly held companies or private equity groups. Inability to find qualified personnel. These are a few of the dynamics that are common in changing industries.

In the old days, you had the fortitude, energy, and enthusiasm to deal with these types of changes in a positive way. You fought – and won – most of the battles. Do you still have the persistence, determination, and money to face the changes in your industry that are on the horizon?

If such ideas are no longer exciting, perhaps it's time for you to "cash out."

If these ideas excite you and you'd like to be a part of the changes, but you're uncertain about the economic outcome, perhaps you need to seek a strategic buyer who'll retain you with an employment contract.

Do I plan to retire in the near future?

One of the most common reasons for selling a company is to provide a business owner with a viable income to use during retirement. Even though your earlier plans may have included having your son, daughter, or even your favorite nephew take over your business, the days of "following in the old man's footsteps" are less frequent.

Business dynasties, like those immortalized by the Fords and the Rockefellers and the Watsons, are but a page turn in the history books. Many of today's independent offspring are busy making their own fortunes and names, rather than accepting the key to the executive washroom from Dear Old Dad or Mom.

Like it or not, you will come to face two realities: a) You aren't going to live forever; and b) Junior doesn't want to sit in your chair.

With these ideas in mind, many company owners decide that comfortable retirement can occur only after a comfortable sale of the business.

Are the key decision makers in my company moving in the right direction?

If you are in a business with another owner, you may be experiencing a sense of loss or indifference that was not present in the "we can take over the world" stage of your entrepreneurial partnership. In those days, small differences and disagreements were easily handled by certain pacifiers in the form of bonuses, perks, or larger office square footage. But now, you're no longer the new kids.

In fact, those new kids have grown to have kids, spouses, and debts of their own.

In many businesses partnerships, strategic decisions involving marketing, planning, and expansion lead to some heated family and financial feuds – often resulting in the partners deciding to sell the company.

Does my business offer a specialty product or service that a larger company wants?

Perhaps your decision to sell the business is prompted by the request of someone for you to do so. If your company is successful (and oftentimes, even if it's not!), there's someone out there in this vast world who wants to buy it. The old adage, "Everything's for sale," is certainly true when it comes to businesses. This is especially true if your business offers some type of specialty or niche service or product.

If your business offers something that is popular in a small but expanding market, then you should expect that tap on the shoulder from a prospective buyer – if he hasn't already knocked you over with phone calls, e-mails, luncheon invitations, or neatly written, yet legalized, pleas saying, "Please, please, please let me buy you." (Well, not exactly in those words, but with enough of an eye twinkle to let you know that the interest is definitely genuine.)

If you're a manufacturing business with a unique product in a niche market, then you may be a large target in the sights of a foreign firm.

If the niche product that you produce can be easily added to the product line of another company and pushed through the distribution network for lower marketing costs than you are expending, then you might as well be wearing a bull's-eye. In this case, THEY want YOU.

The key thing is niche. If you make a product that fits a niche, you may want to be prepared to be sold rather than to be swallowed whole by a "bigger fish" without warning, and at a lower price than you might otherwise command.

Do I need to sell this business to make room or to raise cash for my other interests?

In a decade of economic turmoil and uncertainty, you may decide to sell your business in whole or in part to raise capital for other business ventures. As the economy and customer demands change, you may realize that one aspect of your business is more essential (a bigger contributor to the bottom line) than another aspect of the business. In these cases, it may be necessary to expand Part A by selling Part B.

The need for capital investment and improvements in one part of the business often can be resolved by putting another aspect of the company onto the selling block.

Am I faced with a personal challenge, such as an illness or prospective divorce?

An unplanned change in personal circumstances often triggers the desire, or necessity, to sell an independently owned company.

Why am I doing this?

The ideas just presented are the most common reasons to sell a business. Yours may be different. However, whatever your reason, or your motivation, you have to ask yourself an important question:

Why am I doing this?

Is your motivation to sell your business for the most money that you can? Is it to continue what you believe is a very high quality organization and you want to do everything to maintain that quality and service? Is it important that the employees you nurtured, with whom you grew up and feel very close to, are "taken care of?" Or is your attitude more, "I really don't care about any of this – I just want to get out of it while I can" state of mind?

Regardless, you need to answer the question, "Why am I doing this?" You have to make sure that you maintain your focus on your answer throughout the process of the sale. In the months and decisions ahead, there will be a vast amount of time-consuming activities all needing your immediate attention. By keeping your prime focus on your answer to "Why am I doing this?" you'll be able to see the light, the dollar signs, and the sense of security that led you to this path in the first place.

Because it is so important, please take the time to think about your answer now, and write it down. While you're mulling over your response, remember to be precise.

So, fire up your word processor and at the top of a blank page put the words:

TODAY'S DATE:

HERE'S WHY I WANT TO SELL MY COMPANY:

Now list the reasons. (If you're not computer literate, just use a piece of paper... and write everything using ink.)

And while you are in a creative mode, think about this question: What do I want my role to be after the business is sold? Do I want to be a beach bum, an independent consultant, a freelance writer, or a highly skilled and highly paid employee of the new owner? Headline another page:

HERE'S WHAT I WANT MY ROLE TO BE AFTER THE SALE.

Now make a list.

Don't lose these written statements!

OK. You've written it down. Congratulations. You now have permission to do three things:

    1. Exercise the emotion of your choice. You can laugh, cry, take a deep breath, say a prayer, holler an expletive remark. You're entitled. Deciding to sell your business is an emotional big deal. The baby you gave birth to –

raised, sweat blood over, lost sleep about – is one day going to belong to somebody else.
2. Keep the written statement of WHY you want to sell your business in a safe yet accessible place. As you read earlier, the activities in the next few months may coax you to lose sight of why you reached this decision point – so keep the reminder handy.
3. Move forward…with caution. If you're like most people, once you've made up your mind to sell – even if you're still having the "maybe I ought to" conversation with yourself – your focus could turn away from growing the business as you concentrate on moving the sale process forward. Perish such thoughts! Now is definitely not the time to become complacent about the continued success of your company. Be aware that the value of your business will decrease with your level of enthusiasm about your business.

So, if you've made the decision to sell, move forward by making plans to do it. The purpose of this book is to help guide you through the process.

Perspective of a contributing writer...

WHY SELL?

By George Sierchio

Sometimes things happen and you just have to get out. Other times you are just ready for a change of pace. Your enthusiasm to build and work the business isn't really there anymore. Seriously ask yourself if you are still at least 75 percent as enthusiastic about building the business as you were in year one or two when you started. If you are like many people, you have done your best in the business for three-plus years and don't have the desire to make it any better, or you really are ready to move on to the next business you want to build. Maybe it is time to just retire. That's something you certainly have to ask yourself every year that you are in business.

Here are the best reasons to discretely put your business on the market and attract a buyer:

- You are bored with the business (but it's doing well).
- The business is no longer satisfying to deal with every day (but it's doing well).
- It's built up enough to cash out.
- You found something more exciting to be a part of.
- You really do wish to retire.

The truly best time to sell a business is when it is making good money and you don't absolutely NEED to get out. This principle holds true for most things dealing with money: It comes much easier when you don't desperately need it. Ask your bank when the best time is to go for a loan. I promise your bankers will tell you, "Whenever it's not necessary to have it."

If you happen to be in a bad position such as a divorce, partner dispute, or illness, then you probably can't expect to get top dollar for your company. But I promise you that you won't get much at all if you don't use professional help to sell. Smart buyers will see your desperation very quickly if they are dealing with you one-on-one because there is no buffer between you and them. You will be fighting a losing battle.

Courtesy of George Sierchio, Accredited Business Coach, Seasoned Buy/Sell Intermediary, Speaker, and Author
Action Business Partners, Inc.
P.O. Box 5454
Parsippany NJ 07054
Phone: 973-394-9800
E-mail: info@actionbusinesspartners.com
Web: http://actionbusinesspartners.com/

Perspective of a contributing writer...
CASE STUDY

FAT, DUMB AND HAPPY

By Andrew Rogerson, CBI

This real-life business story is interesting for two reasons. First is its simplicity. Second, I suspect it's a situation that could happen to any business owner, or perhaps more importantly, should be something every business owner proactively works to avoid happening to his or her business.

This business is an electrical wholesale distribution business in Sacramento, Calif. The business was established in 1954 by the current owner's father. The current owner was in his mid 50s. He grew up in the business and when the time was right, took over its ownership. The good news for the owner was that he worked only about five hours a week. This allowed him to spend time on his ranch with his wife and family as well as his nearby grandchildren.

Because he grew up in the industry, he knew all the products, all the local industry players, and his accounting background allowed him to manage his business from the reports he received.

The day-to-day running of the business was handled by two very experienced managers. One of the managers was approaching 70, but was a ball of energy, had been in the industry for more than 40 years, loved what he did, and had an unprecedented level of knowledge and connections. His primary focus was sales, connecting with owners and other tradesmen, and staying on top of government contracts so the company could competitively bid and bring in new business. The other manager was a knowledge maven, had great organizational skills, and was responsible for overseeing a team of about 19 full-time employees and 3 part-timers, chasing the best prices and simply getting it done.

If you looked at the raw gross sales of the business, business was good. From 2004 to 2007, the gross sales were $5.4 million, $6.393 million, $6.77 million, and $8.35 million, respectively. In 2008, the company was projected to finish the year at about the same as 2007 – in a difficult local, regional, national and global economy, most business owners would be delighted to get that result.

The owner of the business was also fortunate that he owned the land and buildings. The main building the business operated from was about 9,000 square feet, plus there was about another 11,000 square feet of space.

In early December 2008, I received a phone call from the owner. He decided he had to sell the business. It was a great deal. All the owner wanted was the buyer to pay for the current value of the inventory, which he thought was about $850,000. Everything was included in the price: the business name; all employees; a complete list of furniture, fixtures and equipment; and all the inventory with the accounts receivable and accounts payable negotiable. The land and buildings were not part of the sale, but could be bought as a separate transaction, or the seller was prepared to offer six months' free rent.

The opportunity for me to sell the business only came with one caveat: I had to find a buyer for him by Christmas or he was closing the doors. In other words, I had three weeks to market the business, qualify suitable buyers, write an offer, complete due diligence, and close escrow.

So what was troubling this business that the owner wanted to sell in three weeks or close the door? I guess the problem could be defined in a couple of ways, but the best definition came from the owner. As he said, "I became Fat, Dumb, and Happy." He became Fat, Dumb, and Happy because he took his eye off the ball. The business had all the right ingredients – longevity and market share (in business 50-plus years), low overhead (owned the land and the buildings and bought their goods from the largest buying consortia for their industry in the United States), well-trained, knowledgeable, and motivated employees (absentee owner that worked five hours per week), and loyal customers (sales were growing or holding in a difficult local economy).

However, when I asked if I could get a report for the company's last inventory count so I could show potential buyers, it turned out there had been no true inventory count for many years. In addition, when I went to look over the business, there was inventory everywhere. Much of it, which I confirmed with the owner, might have been out of date and therefore worth pennies on the dollar.

From my perspective, the problem for this business was threefold.

First, the Accounts Receivables ballooned, and ballooned quickly, because not enough attention was being paid. Instead of the business withdrawing credit from the slow-paying customers, it became a bank. Just like any bank, if withdrawals exceed deposits, the bank is closed down. This is what happened to this business.

Secondly, the owner lost his hunger to work in the business. He had two other businesses within walking distance of this business, and they were being run by some of his children. As a result, he had little day-to-day knowledge of what was happening. When he was finally brought up to speed, the business had reached a negative tipping point and it was unable to recover.

Third, and I think most importantly, the owner of the business lost what I believe is the core responsibility of the owner of a business, and that is to provide its vision. I spent more than 15 hours trying to help the owner of this business solve his problem.

I brought two qualified buyers who had an interest in trying to do something. One buyer was heavily involved in construction and so saw great value in buying the business and using it to get the best pricing on electrical goods. A second buyer saw the "green" potential of the business. The business had a strong footprint in the local market, but was not carrying any "green" or energy-efficient products. This buyer saw a whole new opportunity of sales that the current owner considered, but had been too Fat, Dumb, and Happy to drill down and understand. And interestingly enough, the buying consortia he was part of had the most advanced range of energy-efficient products at the best prices. It would have been a fairly easy transition to carry this product line.

As I mentioned earlier, there are two simple things to learn from this situation.

The first is that the pre-eminent responsibility of the owner, president, or CEO of the business is to provide the vision of the enterprise. It's a given that the global, national, regional, and local economies are always in motion. As they say, change is inevitable. However, only one person can provide the vision and this must fall to the owner. To quote George Washington Carver, "Where there is no vision there is no hope."

The second lesson concerns the personal energy of the owner. Running a business, at a minimum, requires energy, attention to detail, and a plan. If the owner wants to spend as little time in the business as possible, then I would suggest the owner start building and executing an exit strategy.

In my opinion and from what I see working as a business broker, far too many business owners leave or sell their business too late. As a result, employees become jaded because they don't think ownership cares enough, suppliers start getting paid late and become concerned, and customers don't get the attention they have come to expect. The slow decline starts building momentum, which ultimately results in a lower selling price for the business, if a willing buyer comes along at all.

Selling a business is not a quick process. I would suggest it takes at least 12 months. For a more complex business, it may take up to three years.

Selling a company also includes using professional assistance to coordinate and manage the different areas of selling a business, such as the marketing of the business; handling the legal contracts; negotiations with different parties, including the buyers, landlords, accounting and legal parties; and ensuring the business is protected from nosy "tourists" who have no interest other than wanting to know what's going on.

What's the best time to start considering an exit strategy? That answer is easy. Each successful company has a business plan. It should be standard operating procedure to do an annual review of the business to see if the goals for the previous year were met. If goals were met, how and why were they achieved? If not, same question.

With the review of the business plan comes forward planning. This is the time to consider an exit plan for the owner of the business. If the business plan is to move onward and forward for the next 12 months, then a plan with any changes will evolve. Understanding those changes, be they subtle or dramatic, demands attention. Once they are understood, those changes need to be communicated and executed. The changes may demand that the business be downsized until the next opportunity is clearly identified. Alternatively, it may mean retraining some or all of the team for the next opportunity.

Inaction or lack of attention is not an option. In the owner's words, being Fat, Dumb, and Happy won't work. By its very nature, the capitalist system doesn't reward or tolerate that behavior.

Courtesy of Andrew Rogerson,
Certified Business Intermediary (CBI)
Murphy Business and Financial Corporation –
   N CA
777 Campus Commons Road, Suite 200
Sacramento, CA 95825
Phone: 916-570-2674
E-mail: a.rogerson@murphybusiness.com
Web: http://www.Andrew-Rogerson.com

CHAPTER TWO

Getting the Right Help

Getting the Right Help

For Sale by Owner?

Even though you are no doubt an amazing person, you have to admit (at least in the privacy of your own head) that you can't do EVERYTHING. Otherwise, you'd have no employees, no buyers, no suppliers, and no worries.

But that's not the case.

Once you have made the decision to sell your business, you have to pull in some helpers who will enable you to do it. Sure, this will cost money. In the long-run, the upfront investment that you make will lead to a greater payoff in the end. (Doesn't that sound like something you have said before?) It's good advice.

Remember the old saying, "A doctor who performs surgery on himself has a fool for a patient"? This adage can also be applied to a business owner who intends to sell his own company.

The fact is that a person who is good (even outstanding) at owning or running a business can't really be skilled at selling that same business. Sure, you can sell the goods and services that the business makes – but you can't sell the business itself. There are several reasons for this:

    1. Your emotions. Even though you may be the kind of person who is very skilled at keeping your reactions in

check, when it comes to your little slice of the American Dream, you're bound to be emotional.
2. Your judgment. You might think that your business is a gold mine. It may very well be. However, the price of gold in your head might be a little bit different than the price of gold in the buyer's head. This isn't to say that yours is too high and his is too low; in fact, it may be just the opposite, but opposites don't seem too attractive in a buy/sell situation.
3. Your contacts. If you had to sell your business today, who would be the first person you'd approach to buy it? Most business owners will list a competitor, an employee, a customer, or a supplier. Did you?

    If you did, you're in good company with most business owners, but you're thinking too small, too local. The world is a great big place.
4. Your reference point. You are not the buyer. There is really no way to clearly understand his motive for buying your business unless you can slip into his psyche – or engage the services of someone who makes deals for a living.
5. Your educational background. Let's guess. You don't have a law degree, right? Selling anything with the magnitude of your business requires the engagement of a legal professional who knows what the fine print really says. And while you're wondering why you did make the career choice that you did, you also need to strongly consider the services of a financial expert in business sales. Besides knowing all about debits and credits, this professional can help you navigate the ever-changing Internal Revenue Service requirements for transactions of this nature.

Selling a company can be an intricate and time-consuming task. There are legal, accounting, tax, and regulatory issues to deal with. Further, there is the task of finding a qualified buyer, then negotiating and structuring the deal to your best advantage. Also, if you plan the sale as a "do-it-yourself project," who is going to continue to run your company on a day-to-day basis – keeping it successful – while you work on all of the details required during the sales process? From beginning to end, the project may take as long as a year to complete.

Perspective of a contributing writer...
CASE STUDY

MY FIRST RADIO SHOW
By Scott D. Mashuda, CBI

I submitted an entry to my Company blog attacking a powerful local business radio show host. The piece was titled, "WARNING: Radio Host Ron Morris, 'The American Entrepreneur,' is Misinformed and Misguiding His Listeners On How To Sell Their Businesses!"

Ron Morris is not your average radio show host. He is a 10-time entrepreneur over a 35-plus year professional career. He is the founder and director of the Entrepreneurial Studies Program at Duquesne University. He is an advisory board member for the National Foundation for Teaching Entrepreneurship and the founder or co-founder of many prominent Western Pennsylvania businesses, including:
- Pittsburgh Business Radio
- IGATE Capital (formerly Mastech)

- Rapidigm (formerly ComputerPeople)
- MestMed
- JD Warren Inc.

Why then would I make such an outrageous comment and create controversy with such an accomplished individual? Plain and simple, I had to protect my turf!

Here's the whole story...

Ron Morris, the "American Entrepreneur," on his American Entrepreneur Radio show, received a call from an entrepreneur and avid listener named Yuri. Yuri recalled Ron's statement from a previous broadcast, declaring, "It is a bad idea to use a business broker to sell your business." Yuri's question: "Why?"

Ron's response provided yet another black eye to a profession that has been at times fairly, but mostly unfairly, bruised and battered. His basic argument to Yuri was that you should not use a business broker to handle the sale of your business because the fee you are required to pay is not in line with the service you will receive. Ron argued that the local business broker community was not a professional and qualified group and that the transaction would be just as successful if Yuri coupled his own efforts with those of his accountant and attorney. In my opinion, this advice was misinformed, misguided, and reckless.

The cost of NOT hiring a business broker FAR EXCEEDS the cost of hiring one. There is no active market in which ownership in a closely held business is traded. Unlike owning stock in a publicly traded company such as Wal-Mart or Microsoft, you cannot simply call your broker or click a button to sell your independently owned business. A market for your business must be created from scratch.

Ron's argument that you can create this market yourself is the classic build-versus-buy dilemma. As with any product or service that you purchase from a retailer or service provider, you must make the decision either to buy the product/service or build/create/provide the product or service yourself. Consider a few examples: Should you buy a house or build a house? Should you hire an accountant to prepare your tax returns or self-prepare? Should you see a heart specialist for chest pain or go to medical school and fix it yourself?

If you are an expert in any of these areas, you may elect to go at it alone. If not, then you either need to learn how to do them or pay a fee to have someone else do them for you. If you elect to learn them yourself, you may in time be extremely successful. However, it will take time (and lots of it) to obtain the experience of an expert. The only way you will avoid making mistakes in your new endeavor is to be an expert. The only way you will become an expert is to make mistakes.

Chances are you only have one business. You only have one shot to sell your business. It is in all likelihood the largest asset that you own and the backbone of your retirement plans. Therefore, there is no margin for error. If you don't sell your business at its highest potential price the first time around, you have no second chance.

To maximize your potential for success you must surround yourself with the right team of good people. This team consists of your accountant, a transaction attorney (both as suggested by Ron), AND a business broker.

The most common mistakes suffered by those who fail to use a business broker:

• Confidentiality Breach. Confidentiality is crucial! Your employees receiving word that they may not have a job in six months because you are looking to sell is business suicide. If word reaches your vendors that you are looking to sell, they will almost certainly stop extending you credit and require cash on delivery. If word reaches your customers that you are looking to sell, sales in all likelihood will plummet while customers wonder if you will be there to support your products or services in six to 12 months. What an edge you just handed your competition!

• Lower Sales Price. Determining the proper asking price for your business is one of the key elements in generating interest from potential buyers. Price it wrong and it will sit on the market and rot.

• Time Commitment. Selling your business takes time. Doing it yourself takes time away from running your business. This change of focus from running to selling means your business will not receive the time and attention that is required to keep cash flow at a level that supports the highest possible selling price.

As I have stated on many occasions, the question that needs to be asked is not "Should I use a business broker?" That answer is a loud and resounding "YES!" The question that needs to be asked is "How do I select the BEST business broker to handle the sale of my business?" Unfortunately, just as there are bad accountants and bad doctors, there are bad business brokers. It is imperative that you find the best broker before selling your business.

To my surprise and good fortune, a few weeks after making this blog post, the phone rang in my office. The voice on the other end said, "This is Ron Morris and I read your blog." I almost fell off my seat! My mind was racing.

Ron continued, "Scott, obviously we don't agree on this subject, but that makes for great radio. Why don't you come on the show and we'll debate this." Oh wow! This is not what I expected, but exactly what I wanted: a chance to set the record straight and educate the local business community on the merits of a good business broker.

So I accepted. The question that remained was, "Would I be afforded the opportunity to present my position in an educated and informed manner, or would this be a childish ego-driven mud-slinging contest in which each party refused to surrender their position?"

As I drove to the radio station that day, I was beaming with confidence and excited to tell the local business community why my profession was integral to the successful transfer of their business interests. So, I kicked on the radio to hear the prelude. Ron was telling the story of how we met through the blog post and preparing his listeners for a "battle."

OK, now I was nervous. This was my first time making an appearance on live radio and I was about to defend a profession in which public perception was squarely not in my corner. I knew that, but I also knew that my firm was different. We were not what was "wrong" with the business brokerage profession. We are everything that is "right" about the profession. I needed to let it be known that good business brokers, like us, do exist. I needed to convince Ron.

When I arrived at the radio station, I could not have been more surprised and more pleased. Ron approached me with a big smile, stuck out his hand and said, "Don't be nervous about all the hype. That's for the listeners. I did my homework on you and your firm. You have the credentials. You have the experience. And, if you are what you say you are, I am impressed. Now, let's demonstrate that to my listeners!"

So, the show went "live." It was not a battle, but rather an informed and educated discussion. Ron knew from his research how we were different and he allowed me the opportunity to address each one of the concerns he had presented on the previous show. He made this show about me, my credentials, my company and our credentials, not about him. Our discussion was informative, professional, civil, and educational. Ron Morris was a true class act!

In the end, Ron and I became good friends. My firm, River's Edge Alliance Group, became a sponsor of his Pittsburgh Business Radio Show and I have since served as an adjunct professor at Duquesne University teaching "Financing, Valuing and Exiting Your Business" as part of Ron's entrepreneurial studies program.

Courtesy of Scott D. Mashuda,
Certified Business Intermediary (CBI)
River's Edge Alliance Group, LLC
PO Box 24553

Pittsburgh, PA 15234
Phone: 412-894-3244
E-mail: smashuda@RiversEdgeAlliance.com
Web: http://www.RiversEdgeAlliance.com/

The cost of selling a business

Another thing that you may have in common with other business owners is your dislike of paying professional fees for accountants, attorneys, and consultants. You want to engage the services of these professionals only when it is "absolutely necessary." Selling your business is one of those absolutely necessary times, because the sale of your company could well be the most important economic decision you make in your entire life. In fact, you will need to budget for the services of three selling professionals:

1. Someone to make it legal.
2. Someone to make it lucrative.
3. Someone to make it happen.

Someone to make it legal

Most companies have a corporate lawyer or a corporate law staff. These people have become your trusted allies over the years, helping you avoid crises and making sure that everyday dealings with leases, operating agreements, and employee benefits were handled in the most upright, by-the-book manner. They may even be your friends. So, keep them out of your deal – unless they have a track record of selling businesses.

This isn't to say that they are not qualified. They are – for legal issues concerning ongoing business operations. But how experienced are they at selling a business? How many businesses have they sold? For this venture, you need a specialist.

As you know, attorneys – like physicians – specialize in various fields. Some specialize in bankruptcy law, criminal defense law, labor law, employment law, environmental law, or real estate law.

You need a "business transaction attorney," one who specializes mostly in corporate law, with a majority of his billable hours being invoiced for work with mergers and acquisitions.

When considering a firm to handle your transaction, ask these questions:

"How many deals of my size (based on annual revenue) have you done in the last five years?"

"How about in the last 12 months?"

Then, ask around and make sure.

Remember that there are lawyers and then there are deal lawyers. The latter is more like a facilitator – someone you engage to protect your interests and to effect the sale. A deal lawyer has been through hundreds of deals. The buyer of your company has been through dozens of deals. How many deals has your company attorney done? How many have you done?

What's a lawyer to do?

If engaged early in the process, the lawyer can outline the steps you will need to follow to protect yourself and to make sure that the deal runs smoothly. Your attorney will also know about the transferability of any leases or other agreements that the buyer will have to obtain before the deal can close.

Later in the process, the lawyer will be essential in reviewing the purchase agreement and sales agreement. He will also be necessary to handle the details of closing the deal.

As a general rule, don't sign anything before having your attorney read it first.

Someone to make it lucrative

Another aspect of selling your business involves taxation. By asking some of the same questions that you posed to the attorney, you can make certain that your current tax advisor is up-to-date and qualified to address the legalities of the Internal Revenue Service. As you've realized through other transactions with your business, you've always had a silent partner – the IRS. And it will be there when you sell your business, silently salivating for its slice of your all-American pie.

Many larger law firms and public accounting firms – especially in metropolitan areas – have specialists on staff who concentrate on issues of corporate taxation. Be sure that your tax advisor is competent and experienced in tax matters relating to the sale of your company.

Sometimes you can hire an attorney whose firm specializes in both mergers and acquisitions, and the tax laws related to them. Though you'll be billed for all services, this is better than a "buy one – get one free" because the logistics of your deal can be more easily coordinated.

If you're still wavering about using the already-retained services of your company's attorney and accountant – the lawyer who keeps the corporate minute book up-to-date and the accountant who does your quarterly and yearly tax filings – think about this: These advisors and their firms have been billing your company quite handsomely for years. Working for you is their way of life. Once the deal is done, your business will no longer be a participant in their billing and accounts receivable programs. In plain language, it clearly may not be in their best interests for you to sell your company. This explains why they could find all kinds of points to pick apart during the deal you're trying to make with a buyer.

Your motives and theirs are not the same.

What's an accountant to do?

Your tax accountant will be able to explain the tax consequences of the sale and some of the possible alternatives for structuring the deal.

He will also be responsible for producing financial statements that will put your company in the best light for the buyer – a little bit different from presenting your numbers for income tax filing. Talk with your accountant about producing statements on the accrual rather than cash basis, and other possible modifications that would strengthen your financial statements without red-flagging suspicion or crossing the line of acceptable accounting practices.

Someone to make it happen

Many people out there will claim that they can successfully sell your company. Just make sure that this is more than a claim. For the person you choose, it should be his way of life.

The official title of this advisor is "intermediary," although in practice this person is a merger and acquisition consultant or facilitator. An intermediary will be the person who will find the right buyer for your business. He will be involved in the process of helping you value your business, evaluating potential buyers, negotiating the terms, and properly structuring the deal in your best interest.

A good intermediary knows how to research your specific industry as well as related industries to determine who is "right" for buying your company. He will screen potential buyers to ensure that they are suitable and qualified – both professionally and financially – to look at your deal. Before revealing the name of your company to a potential suitor, your intermediary will ask the individual (or company) to submit a confidential buyer/investor profile. In the profile, the potential buyer will be asked about his background and the reasons why he may be interested in buying a company such as yours. The potential buyer will also be asked to reveal his liquidity, net worth, financial statements, and a description of the sources of funding he intends to use to finance the deal. Requiring potential buyers to submit to such scrutiny early in the process usually discourages insincere or unqualified individuals or companies. It weeds out those "tire kickers" who may have no professional expertise or financial wherewithal to finalize a deal.

An intermediary will have extensive contacts with other merger and acquisition professionals throughout the world who know of qualified buyers that may be interested in what your company has to offer.

This advisor will be a good business professional. He will focus on your needs and how to fill them.

The first order of business for this consultant will be the preparation of a confidential evaluation of your business – used as an in-house working tool only – highlighting the key information needed to obtain the most professional and profitable sale.

This evaluation will include:

1. The strengths of your business and how to maximize them.
2. The earnings potential of the business, based on an in-depth analysis of the market.
3. The fair market value of your business and its potential returns to the buyer.

This evaluation will be for your eyes only, so you can begin to see your business through the view of a potential buyer. Later, as your relationship with the intermediary develops – and as you begin to focus on specifics of the deal – other evaluations will be prepared and shared with the prospective buyer.

What's an intermediary to do?

A good intermediary will be able to advise you on most aspects of the sale of your business. This will include the value, marketing strategies, economic conditions affecting the sales climate, etc. You may also find that the intermediary has a ready buyer for the business.

Keeping the confidence

With all advisors you choose, you'll want to make sure that you've selected ones whom you can trust and respect – ones you are comfortable working with and who are comfortable working with each other. You need to make a subjective judgment that the "chemistry" between you and each of them is "right." Most deals of your size may take up to a year to complete, so you want to make certain that there is a mutual level of comfort and a key goal shared by all the players.

You'll also want to discuss the subject of confidentiality with all of your outside resources, especially your intermediary. Because he will be contacting many companies (and giving them financial details about your business), you will need to know how he plans to contact prospective buyers and still maintain your confidentiality.

At some point in the process, a prospective buyer will be asked to sign a Confidentiality Agreement or a Non-Disclosure Agreement. These can be written very simply or in tedious detail. The choice is yours. Your intermediary probably has one that will serve your purposes.

All confidentiality agreements need to contain these essential elements:

1. A confirmation of the entities who are a part of the agreement.
2. A definition of "information" that is being supplied.
3. Why the information is being furnished.
4. A definition of whose rights are being protected by the agreement.
5. An understanding that all information – including photocopies or electronic copies – shall be promptly returned or destroyed, as directed by the seller.
6. An understanding that the agreement is for confidentiality purposes only, and it is in no way intended to contain representations or warranties.

As an option, you may wish to include in the agreement a clause containing a restriction that prevents the reader from entering your current market for a year if the deal does not go through. This provides you with some protection in the event that the buyer decides yours is a lucrative market and decides to compete against you after reviewing the information you provide. Such a clause, of course, becomes problematic if the potential buyer is already a competitor in your market area.

Paying now instead of later

Again, it needs to be emphasized that this is not the place to scrimp. You need to hire the best advisors, and the best advisors cost money.

Some merger and acquisition advisors are paid a success fee when the deal closes and nothing but out-of-pocket expenses if it doesn't. The fee is usually a percentage of the total selling price. Other advisors may charge an hourly fee; still others may charge on a project basis. However, fees for professional services are negotiable and need to be agreed upon in writing when hiring the advisor. This can be done using a formal contract or letter of engagement.

Check them out

Don't hurry the process. Interview several candidates as diligently as you would when hiring a key player for your business. (In reality, you are!)

Remember to ask these questions:
1. How many years of experience do you have?
2. How many years of experience do you have in this particular area?
3. How many buying or selling deals, or transactions, have you done?
3. Would you feel comfortable representing my interests?
4. Why would you be a good advisor for me?
5. What is your workload right now and in the immediate future?
6. What fee do you charge? (Don't forget to ask about additional expenses, such as phone and fax charges, travel and lodging, photocopying, electronic scanning, and printing.)
7. How will I be kept informed of your progress?
8. How will confidentiality be maintained?
9. How can our agreement be ended?

Your commitment

Most advisors will want to know what they can expect from you in return for their services. Be sure to let them know your plans to:
1. Be honest and open about every fact concerning your business situation, whether favorable or unfavorable.
2. Be prepared for all of your meetings, bringing the necessary information, documents, questions, and answers.

3. Adhere to deadlines, especially when certain information is required by a certain date.
4. Be open about any dissatisfaction you may have with the work of any advisor.

Perspective of a contributing writer...

SELECTING THE BEST BUSINESS BROKER TO SELL YOUR BUSINESS
By Scott D. Mashuda, CBI

As the managing director of a Pittsburgh-based lower-middle market mergers and acquisitions firm, I hold a unique perspective on the business transaction marketplace, the advisors offering you their services, and the questions you should be asking to make sure that you hire the RIGHT business broker/intermediary to represent your business for sale.

The most important thing to remember when interviewing potential business brokers is that it is the job of whomever you hire to create a market for and ultimately sell your business. This may seem rudimentary. However, it must remain at the core of your broker selection process to assure the best intermediary is hired to represent your business for sale.

Does the person you are interviewing have the ability to successfully create a competitive market for your business and secure the best possible buyer for the business? Unlike owning stock in public corporations, real estate, and/or other investment vehicles where an active, public market exists to divest your ownership share, no readily available market currently exists for the ownership transfer of your privately held business. Therefore, it is the fundamental responsibility of the representative you hire to create that market for you.

How do you determine if the individual or firm you are interviewing possesses the ability to create an active market for your business?

Here's where I suggest you concentrate your efforts:

How does the business broker or intermediary plan to market your business for sale? Will he simply post it on the Internet and hope that it sells? If this is the case, I strongly suggest you consider another direction. Successful intermediaries will take an active approach to selling your business. In addition to listing the business for sale on available Internet sites, successful representatives will:

- Contact strategic industry buyers, confidentially inquiring about their interest in a potential acquisition.
- Present your business to an internally maintained database of financial and strategic buyers.
- Contact other local professionals (accountants, attorneys, etc.) to provide them with a confidential overview of the businesses they are offering for sale and inquire if any prospective clients may have an interest.
- Work with other business broker/intermediaries to cross-pollinate deal flow. Example: If an

intermediary from ABC Business Brokerage is working with a buyer for a distribution company and another business broker from XYZ Business Brokerage is working with the seller of a distribution company, only the intermediaries working together will uncover the fit. Not all brokers will cooperate with other intermediaries. Make sure yours will.

Now for my list of cautions:

- Do not get hung up on the business broker's experience within your industry. Any intermediary worth his commission that does not currently possess experience within your industry will seek it. The importance of industry experience will vary depending on the industry and size of the business. However, it is important to recognize that industry experience is secondary to whether you believe in the intermediary's ability to successfully create a market and consummate a sale for your business.

- Price should not be the determining factor on whom you hire. Remember the old adage, "You get what you pay for?" Don't learn this lesson while selling the biggest and most valuable asset that you own! Work through the process detailed above and hire the best person for the job, not the cheapest.

- Don't have the person selling the business be the one to appraise the value. I have seen a lot of brokers attempt to value businesses. My advice is to be cautious with this approach. Unless your business is so small that there is no benefit to hiring an accredited, independent third party for the valuation, I would recommend you do so. Knowledgeable buyers will not find comfort in a value derived by your hired representative. An independent, certified, third party is a must. Accrediting agencies include: The American Society of Appraisers, The Institute of Business Appraisers, and The American Institute of Certified Public Accountants.

Your business is, for all intent and purposes, the largest and most valuable asset that you own. Selling it can be a highly emotional and stressful process. When selecting a representative to handle the sale, take the time to interview multiple intermediaries. Compare and contrast their styles, methodologies, and work ethics. Don't get blinded by the cost, as most good intermediaries will easily pay their own fees through the added value they will bring to your transaction.

And remember: Hire the person you feel is best suited and motivated to generate a market and complete the sale of your business at the maximum potential selling price.

A misconception about hiring multiple brokers:

One of the biggest misconceptions I see with business sellers is that engaging multiple brokers on a nonexclusive basis will increase the likelihood of completing a sale of their business. The theory is that by hiring multiple intermediaries, the business for sale will touch a greater audience, therefore increasing the likelihood of sale.

Although this is great in theory, it is flawed in logic. Even the hardest working and most dedicated brokers have a fixed amount of time and resources to invest in selling your business. There are only 24 hours in a day. Because intermediaries are paid mainly by commission, they are bearing the economic risk for selling your business. It can be argued that without the security of an exclusive agency agreement, the intermediary's risk in a potential transaction will exceed the potential economic benefit.

Example: Let's assume Intermediary A agrees to a nonexclusive agency agreement for XYZ Company. XYZ Company also has nonexclusive agency agreements with Intermediaries B, C, and D. Intermediaries A, B, C, and D are now all assuming 100 percent of the risk on the same transaction. They are each, in essence, agreeing to invest their valuable time, effort, and resources into selling the same business with a maximum 25 percent success rate and a minimum 75 percent failure rate. At best, one will succeed and three will fail.

Now, you may respond with the following, "As long as one succeeds, why do I care?" Or, "I don't care who sells it as long as it sells." However, understand that although brokers and intermediaries are by nature risk takers, they are not fools. They understand that a nonexclusive agency agreement has compounded risk. Therefore, most intermediaries will hedge risk by shifting their limited assets (time, resources, marketing dollars, etc.) to lower risk opportunities (those with exclusive agency).

Just as a buyer will calculate the risk of your business against a potential rate of return, so will a broker assess his risk against his time, effort, and potential rate of return. If the risks of representation exceed the return, the relationship will not succeed and the business will not sell.

If you, as a seller, require an intermediary to assume the economic risk of the transaction, you must be prepared to offer exclusive agency as a hedge.

Courtesy of Scott D. Mashuda,
Certified Business Intermediary (CBI)
River's Edge Alliance Group, LLC
PO Box 24553
Pittsburgh PA 15234
Phone: 412-894-3244
E-mail: smashuda@RiversEdgeAlliance.com
Web: http://www.RiversEdgeAlliance.com/

CHAPTER THREE

Putting a Price Tag on Your Business

Putting a Price Tag on Your Business

Blood, sweat, tears, and dollars

How do you put a price on blood, sweat, and tears? Well, it's not easy.

"Fair market value" is the price that a commodity can bring in an open exchange between buyers and sellers in a free market. The true value of your company can only be determined by the market – and the amount of interest it generates in the market. You may think that your business is worth $15 million, but if the best offer you can get in the market is only $12 million, then it's only worth $12 million.

Putting a dollar value on your business involves a delicate blend of art and science – with the bottom line being the price that the buyer is actually willing to pay. However, just like with a car, a house, or a used piece of equipment, you have to come up with an asking price – not only one you like, but one that you can defend.

That's where your intermediary steps in. His job is to help determine the best method of valuing your business and putting it in the most desirable view for the prospective buyer – despite the external or internal factors at work. Often he will rely upon another professional to conduct an actual "valuation."

What's happening outside your doors?

Even though you might be running a pretty tight ship within the parameters of your control, there are forces beyond your balance sheet that will have an impact on the sale of your business. In an era of economic turmoil, many factors can affect the outcome.

Credit won't be as available to prospective buyers because of the credit crunch. The two prime causes of inflation are excess money growth and credit expansion. When credit limits have been reached – as they are in turbulent economic times – businesses lose their ability to make additional purchases.

Merger and acquisition activity within your industry may affect the price that a buyer is willing to pay for your business. Such activity in an industry tends to follow approximately three-year cycles. When the cycle begins, it is a "seller's market" – there are a few buyers seeking high-quality sellers. High-quality sellers can command higher prices for their companies. More buyers then enter the market and there is heated competition for high-quality sellers. These sellers prosper. As the cycle begins to taper off, the situation begins to change. The best companies have been "cherry-picked" by buyers. Some of these buyers are now content and are no longer in an acquisition mode. The remaining companies for sale – sometimes considered "second tier" because they may not be as high in quality as those that were first purchased – are now sought by fewer buyers. This creates a "buyer's market," where purchase prices offered for the remaining companies are less.

It's about timing

Today, a seller is getting hit hard. First, your earnings may be down. Second, you have buyers who aren't willing to pay what they would have paid several years ago. And third, the buyers who are out there may be bargain hunters.

An ideal time to sell your business is when the economy is growing and the market or industry you represent is expanding. In turn, your sales and profits are up and your next year looks like a winner. In fragmented industries, lots of buyers are accessible in good economic times, looking in full force for businesses where sales and profits are growing.

In these cases, sell the future. Some buyers don't mind a bad past. It's history. What they do mind, however, is an uncertain future – an increase to their risk. It only makes sense that the more predictable you can make your future profits, the less risky the buyer will find the venture, and the more likely he will be to pay your asking price.

The best time to sell is when your company is having a record sales year, with next year looking just as promising.

What goes in affects what goes out

There are several notable factors happening within your company that can greatly affect the price someone is willing to pay for it. These factors are included below in more detail.

Your product or service

In general, your company will be more desirable when it offers a product or service under its own brand name rather than under the name of another company that adds its own label. A buyer recognizes the costly and time-invested process of developing a brand name in both the industrial and consumer markets.

If you can prove the weaknesses of your competitors by documenting how your product or service is better, faster, brighter, and more valuable, then your business becomes better, faster, brighter, and more valuable to the prospective buyer.

Anything that you can do to reduce the unknowns is viewed as a benefit to a smooth and more profitable transaction.

Your management team

In general, companies with well-rounded, experienced, first and second-string management teams are more desirable to a buyer than a one-person operation. The buyer may tend to reduce his purchase price when he identifies the risk of buying out one person and possibly losing his investment if the seller becomes ill, dies, or decides to take his profits and retire.

You will find it easier to sell your business if you have developed a good management team to continue the business operations after you are gone – literally or figuratively.

Your customer base

A business that relies on only a few key customers is worth less than a business with no customer having more than five percent of total sales. In cases where sales are concentrated with a few customers or when customer turnover is high, many buyers will demand that the seller agree to a guaranteed earning level, or to another form of deferred payment based on future earnings.

Your place in the industry

A buyer will pay more for a company whose industry is in a growth trend. Remember to sell the future.

A buyer may also be interested in your company's general reputation in your industry. Is your company regarded as a leader or a laggard? Depending upon the motivation of the buyer, having the status of either may – or may not – be to your advantage.

Your industry in the place

Many buyers don't want to expand your business – at least not immediately following its acquisition. You will be more attractive to a buyer if you can operate at 70 percent of capacity, rather than if you are operating at near or full capacity and therefore require immediate expansion by means of a new or renovated facility.

Your commitment to "just in time"

Buyers and sellers have a very differing view on inventory, especially old inventory. Get rid of slow-moving, outdated, or obsolete inventory. In general, the older the inventory, the less value it has to you as the seller.

Your location

Whether your business' market is regional or national, it will be more salable if it has a positive and strong sales presence in the local arena. This is because mature local markets limit the expansion of many companies. So, look first to your own backyard.

The locations of your suppliers can also influence the sale of your business. If your vendors are nearby, the buyer can correctly assume that it can keep inventory levels down and deliveries timely and reasonably priced. Obviously, this is an attractive feature.

Your research and development efforts

Again, think future. Buyers want to know that you have instilled plans to maintain your company's competitive advantage by investing in development efforts. Sellers will want to see figures answering these questions:

1. How much money are you spending on research and development?
2. What is your company's policy regarding research and development?
3. How many new products or services have been developed over the last five years as a result of research and development efforts?
4. How profitable are these new products or services?

Your employee pension fund

For companies that have pension plans, this is an area of much interest to a prospective buyer. If there is a large deficiency in your company's pension fund reserves, then your deal will not go through – unless you greatly adjust your asking price.

Your balance sheet

The strength of your balance sheet directly affects the value of your business. If your balance sheet conveys a growing and high net worth through its record of hard, fixed assets (machinery, equipment, hardware, vehicles) and makes enough money to finance any improvements, then it's going to be viewed as a winner for the prospective buyer.

Other positive signs that turn on a buyer are accrued liabilities for taxes, sales tax, unused vacation and sick leave, and small pension plan payments that have remained steady over the past two to three years.

Positive signs such as these let the buyer – in a perfect world – know that yours is a good company to buy.

No perfect world

But, as you know, the world is less than perfect.

The most negative sign on your balance sheet (and a red flag to the prospective buyer) is a negative or declining net worth. A buyer may also be uneasy when seeing equipment and vehicles being leased instead of owned by the business. Unless leasing is a common practice in your industry, this may tip off the buyer that the business has cash-flow problems.

Another negative sign, which was addressed earlier, is old or obsolete inventory. This, coupled with long-term debt, clearly spells the message: BUYER BEWARE.

With your accountant, you'll want to look closely at your balance sheet. To keep surprises to a minimum, you may want to upgrade the level of your accounting reports from a "compilation" or "reviewed" status (the simplest kind, with little verification of information by your outside accounting firm) to an "audited" status (where all information on your financial statement is verified by your outside accounting firm).

If your business is showing more negative signs than positive ones, you may want to postpone your plans to sell. In the near term, focus all your attention on straightening out your business and making it one that buyers will want to buy.

How does your business look?

Without peeking at your latest balance sheet, take a few minutes to list the positive and negative attributes of your business. Again, fire up the word processor, and list the POSITIVE POINTS and the NEGATIVE POINTS. This can be used as a preliminary tool in your discussions with your accountant, intermediary, and lawyer. Be honest – at least with yourself and with your advisors.

How much is this business really worth?

The answer to this question is a little different from the answer to the question, "How much do I want to get for the business?"

Although the two may be related – at least in terms of your level of happiness – the standard measure for determining the value of your business is the same as for any exchange of property: Value is what a willing seller and a willing buyer negotiate and agree on at a certain and specified point of time.

In other words, things can change.

One good way for you to maximize the value of your business is to look at future earnings rather than the company's history. The best person to do this is an outside resource.

A valuation from an outside firm goes a long way in convincing a buyer that a fair price has been established. The objectivity of an outside firm makes it much more difficult for a buyer to try to undercut the price, as the buyer can place much more faith in the numbers obtained by an independent resource.

You're too close

Your emotional tie to the business leaves you wearing a set of blinders concerning its value and ultimate worth. Value is subjective. And, like beauty, value is indeed in the eyes of the beholder. Value, then, is an attitude. It is an attitude toward something in view of its estimated capacity to make money.

Is there any wonder why buyers and sellers often disagree about value?

The key thing you'll have to keep in mind is the interest of any buyer: the future economic benefits to be received as a result of this transaction. These benefits can include earnings, cash flow, dividends, or other forms of return on his investment.

It's easy with a crystal ball

The bottom line is that no one knows, with certainty, what the future holds. That's why there are several possible methods to use when determining the value of a company. Working with an outside professional will give you a more in-depth understanding of these methods and assist you in identifying which will give you the greatest satisfaction during the actual transaction.

However, you should be aware of some of the various methods:

1. Capitalized Earnings Method
2. Excess Earnings Method
3. Balance Sheet Method
4. Cost to Create Method
5. Industry Multipliers Method

Capitalized Earnings Method

One of the most commonly used methods of valuing a business is the same method used to value any investments made, such as those concerning stocks, bonds, mutual funds, and savings accounts. Basically, this method refers to the return on investment expected by an investor – in this case, the buyer of your business.

EXAMPLE: Let's say that you have a small, paid-for business that sells walking sticks. For the last 10 years, people have been buying your walking sticks and giving you earnings of $10,100. Your only expense is $100 for office supplies. There has been very little variance in your business, in its flow – and you expect this same rate to continue into the future.

A buyer would look at your walking stick business as being "no risk."

Now, in the real world, there are no "no risk" deals. You take risks, have expenses, and have equipment that depreciates in value. The higher the perceived risk, the higher the capitalization rate (percentage) that the buyer will use to estimate the value of your business.

Rates of 20 percent to 25 percent are common for small business capitalization calculations. This means that buyers will look for a 20 percent to 25 percent return on their investment for buying your business.

The capitalization rate depends on many factors, including the nature of the business and its industry, the stability and predictability of the earnings, and the risk involved. The riskier the business, the higher the capitalization rate. Also, this method does not consider the fair market salary of the future owner or the future earnings of the business or its supporting assets.

Excess Earnings Method

The only difference between this method and the Capitalized Earnings Method is that it splits off return on assets from other earnings. In the case of companies that earn only a small portion of their revenues from tangible assets (such as a service business), the Excess Earnings Method is a good method to use.

The Excess Earnings valuation method is based on return on assets and the income produced by the business. When you invest in an asset, you expect a return on it based on the risk involved. Any return more than the expected return is excess earnings.

This method is easy to use and gives an accurate range of values from which a buyer and seller can negotiate to arrive at a purchase price.

Balance Sheet Method

In some cases, a business is worth no more than the value of its tangible assets. This is true for some businesses that are losing money or paying their owner(s) less than the fair market value for an annual salary. Selling a business like this is often a matter of getting the best possible price for the equipment, inventory, and other tangible assets. However, this is a last resort method to use in valuing your company if your only goal is a quick sale – which is often known as an "Asset Sale."

Cost to Create Method

Some buyers would rather buy your business than start their own. In these cases, it's the buyer who will initiate the use of this valuation method. He will calculate startup needs in terms of dollars and time. Next, he will look at your business and analyze what it has and what it is missing relative to his creation plan. However, this approach is not very common. A company that is profitable will sell for a higher amount than justified by this method. In turn, a business that would sell at this amount (or lower) probably has flaws such as bad location, bad debt, or production problems.

Industry Multipliers Method

In some industries, buyers tend to value a business based upon a multiple of adjusted cash flow or earnings before interest and taxes (known as a "multiple of EBIT").

Interestingly, some industries – especially where the annual sales volume of the average company in the industry is less than one million dollars – have developed other multiplier methods that are commonly relied upon and used when a business is bought or sold. One is the "straight multiplier" method. Some professional advisors are reluctant to use this method because it's usually based on a multiplier of the gross sales, without any value placed on net income, equipment, or other assets. And, because it takes so little effort and is so simple, it gives the appearance of lacking validity. But some industries rely upon this method as the "rule of thumb" when pricing a business.

Pricing resources

Jack Sanders of San Diego, Calif., publishes BIZCOMPS®. It is a database, going back to 1996, designed for accountants, business appraisers, business intermediaries, and their clients. It contains business sales information on "Main Street" companies (i.e., service stations, restaurants, convenience stores, print shops, florists, beauty salons, auto repair shops, day-care centers, etc.). BIZCOMPS® is distributed by Business Valuation Resources, LLC, 1000 S.W. Broadway, Suite 1200, Portland, OR 97205, phone 503-291-7963.

Web: http://www.bizcomps.com/

Many "rule of thumb" pricing formulas for specific businesses are contained in an annual publication titled Business Reference Guide. It contains up-to-date "rules of thumb" and pricing information for more than 500 types of businesses. For more information, contact BUSINESS BROKERAGE PRESS, P.O. Box 218, Wilmington, NC 28402, phone 800-239-5085.

Web: http://www.bbpinc.com/

A common thread

Regardless of the valuation method used, all will have certain things in common: a look at your company's earnings (profits); a look at its cash flow, accounts receivable, allowances for returns or refunds; and a look at its equipment, inventory, furniture, and fixtures. And, of course, a prospective buyer will want to verify the accuracy of all the information you provide.

The defense rests

Because there is no totally objective and surefire way to value a business for buying or selling purposes, you need to make sure you are well prepared to defend your choices of valuation method and asking price. It is not unusual for the buyer to ask you to support the logic behind your asking price. Having a good answer to that question – and a valuation conducted by a professional valuation expert to back you up – will assure the chances of equity and economic satisfaction for all parties.

Perspective of a contributing writer...

UNDERSTANDING THE LANGUAGE
By Scott D. Mashuda, CBI

During discussions to sell your company, you may run into terms that are not familiar to you such as Net Income, EBIT, EBITDA, and SDCF. Having a thorough understanding of these terms and the relationship between them may be the difference between a good financial decision and a bad one.

Net Income. Net income is an accounting term used to define the bottom line of the income statement. It is an accounting concept calculated as follows:

Revenue – (minus) Cost of Goods Sold – (minus) Operating Expenses = Net Income.

Net Income is not the best indicator of a company's true financial performance. Why? Because noncash expenses such as depreciation and amortization are included in the operating expenses that are subtracted from revenue. Depreciation and amortization are theoretical expenses that represent the "using up" of a company's fixed assets (those held on the balance sheet at cost). Since depreciation and amortization are noncash expenses, including them in operating expenses and subtracting them from revenue will help reduce a company's tax obligation, but it will also understate the amount of cash available to a potential buyer.

Net income is influenced not only by cost of goods sold, operating expenses, and non-cash expenses, but also expenses specific to current ownership such as interest expense. Since the current ownership may maintain a level of debt that is not optimal, but specific to their personal situations, interest expense must be stripped out of net income before a company's financial performance can be properly evaluated.

For example, consider a company that is "over-leveraged" (they have more debt on the books than the company can support and manage). This may have occurred simply because the owner has no additional cash or equity to contribute to the business. The company's interest expense under this scenario will exceed that of an owner maintaining a lower level of debt. To evaluate the financial performance of the business, not knowing the financial situation of the current owner, a potential acquirer must strip out interest expenses and concentrate on expenses specific to the business.

Another expense that must be excluded from an acquisition analysis is taxes. If we were to evaluate a company's net income, we would not only be incorrectly evaluating the effects of non-cash expenses on the business (depreciation and amortization) and the impact of the current ownership's financial situation (interest expense), but also a tax effect that is based on a percentage of taxable income number that is already skewed by these expenses (depreciation, amortization, and interest). Since a buyer does not want to evaluate the company to include the current ownership's capital structure in the analysis (interest expense) and their discretionary expenses (to be discussed later), we must move above the tax effect on the income statement to completely strip out their effect (and the effect they have on the company's income tax expense).

EBIT. This is an abbreviation for "Earnings Before Interest and Taxes." EBIT provides a better indication into the true financial performance of a company than net income for all the reasons just mentioned. EBIT is not skewed by the company's tax calculation and the current owner's capital structure. It is one of the best indications of actual operating profit.

Unlike EBITDA (discussed in the next paragraph), EBIT incorporates in its calculation an annual expense allotment for the obsolescence of the company's fixed assets used for revenue producing purposes. This expense takes the form of depreciation for fixed assets and amortization for intangible assets. EBIT is calculated as follows: Net Income + Interest Expense + Income Taxes = EBIT.

EBITDA. This is an acronym for "Earnings Before Interest, Taxes, Depreciation and Amortization."

EBITDA is the best indicator of a company's actual cash performance.

It strips out the company's tax effect, current ownership's capital structure, and eliminates the effect of noncash expenses such as depreciation and amortization.

Rarely does a better metric exist to evaluate the actual cash available to ownership at the end of an operating period to pay down debt, pay taxes, and offer a return to investors than EBITDA. EBITDA is calculated as follows: EBIT + Depreciation + Amortization = EBITDA.

SDCF is an acronym for "Seller's Discretionary Cash Flow." Seller's Discretionary Cash Flow assumes that the owner of the company also works for the business and requires a salary for services performed.

SDCF is calculated as follows: EBITDA + one owner's salary = SDCF. It is important to recognize that SDCF is not the return a buyer will realize for the risk he is taking as an owner or acquirer, but rather the combined return for the duties the owner performs on a day–to-day basis (salary or wages) and the return required for the risk of being the owner.

If SDCF is less than or equal to the salary an owner (or an employee) will require to perform the day-to-day job duties left vacant by the current owner, then the buyer will not be receiving a return for his financial investment. The return will be simply a salary to compensate a buyer for the duties performed as an employee of the business.

Get comfortable with this terminology. You may hear these terms often when during the process of selling your business. You must learn to speak the

language before you can make a reasonably informed and educated selling decision.
  Courtesy of Scott D. Mashuda,
  Certified Business Intermediary (CBI),
  River's Edge Alliance Group, LLC
  PO Box 24553
  Pittsburgh, PA 15234
  Phone: 412-894-3244
  E-mail: smashuda@RiversEdgeAlliance.com
  Web: http://www.RiversEdgeAlliance.com/

Perspective of a contributing writer....

PRICING A CASH-NEGATIVE COMPANY: ASSETS DON'T DICTATE A "BASEMENT" PRICE

By Scott D. Mashuda, CBI

Far too often, business buyers and brokers may rationalize the purchase price of a cash-negative business by the value of the fixed assets available for sale. The argument goes that if the value of the tangible assets is X, the business must be worth at least X because, even on the rainiest day, one could sell these assets to recoup the initial investment.

That is a valid argument only when you have no interest in making money. If you are in the business of making money, you must severely discount the value of these assets because they are not income producing, are illiquid, and come with an opportunity cost.

Buying a business is a risk versus return proposition. The purchased assets must generate a rate of return greater than the buyer's weighted average cost of capital or the assets will cost money rather than make money.

Consider again the cash negative business with a substantial fixed asset base and the buyers that justify an offer price based on the resale value of these assets. Have these buyers considered disposal costs? Carrying costs? Is there even an active market for the resale of these assets? How quickly can they be converted to cash?

I will not argue that a business with breakeven cash flow and a purchase price fully collateralized by the fixed assets presents minimal risk. But I will argue that in most cases it offers minimal return. Risk and return are not mutually exclusive concepts.

To entice investment, the available rate of return on an investment must exceed the rate of return of all other investments with the same risk profile. If a similar return can be achieved elsewhere with less risk, then why would any knowledgeable investor assume the greater risk for less return? This is the concept of opportunity cost.

Now you may argue that the intrigue of the discussed cash negative company, with the purchase price fully collateralized by the assets, is the potential of the assets to eventually generate a return in excess of that available through other investments. This may be a valid argument.

However, you must consider why these assets have potential. Is it because of what you bring to the table as the buyer, or what the seller brings to the table? If you as the buyer create the potential for the assets, then why are you willing to pay the previous owner for this potential?

The seller must bring additional value to the table in excess of the resale value of the fixed assets to justify the full resale value for the assets. Examples include: customer lists, vendor relationships, a talented work force, management team, distribution network, research and development, etc. If there is no additional value offered by the seller, then why should you purchase the fixed assets? Why not purchase a similar set of assets elsewhere (possibly cheaper) with the same ability to produce the desired rate of return? (Hence, your leverage for requiring that the fixed assets be discounted.)

Risk, return, opportunity cost, and asset marketability must be considered in union with each other to properly evaluate the suitability of a potential business acquisition. When doing so, one will quickly ascertain that the fixed assets of a breakeven or cash-negative business do not dictate a "basement" price that a buyer should be willing to pay for the business. If there is no return being offered by the seller to entice an investment in the assets (either monetary or other intangible value), then the buyer should discount the assets. If not, what entices the purchase of these assets? The opportunity to lose money each year?

Courtesy of Scott D. Mashuda,
Certified Business Intermediary (CBI)
River's Edge Alliance Group, LLC

PO Box 24553
Pittsburgh, PA 15234
Phone: 412-894-3244
E-mail: smashuda@RiversEdgeAlliance.com
Web: http://www.RiversEdgeAlliance.com/

CHAPTER FOUR

Preparing a Plan for Selling Your Business

Preparing a Plan for Selling Your Business

Perspective of a contributing writer...
CASE STUDY

SELLER WITH A TIMELINE
By George Sierchio

The owner of a successful engineering consulting business sought my advice on valuing and selling his business. This business was almost 20 years old, had 10 consultants working in it with some support staff, and was fairly streamlined. Its revenues were in line with industry benchmarks as well as the profits. On the surface, all looked good for a nice valuation and a great acquisition target. Except for two problems...

This client of mine had two issues that he needed to get beyond in order to sell for top dollar. First, he waited until he was completely ready to get out before coming up with the idea to sell. It was March and he wanted to be retired by December 31.

His mistake was giving himself a very short timeline to make something happen, something that takes time. It takes time not only to find the correct buyer, but to get the transaction done and to get fully paid. He didn't understand that unlike selling a house, it's very rare, especially in a large transaction, to get paid all at once. And he didn't know that squeezing a time frame often means dropping to a price of less than full value to attract buyers and to make it enticing enough to speed up the sale process.

His second mistake was still being too involved in the sales process. He was the main rainmaker in the business. To a buyer, that spells trouble. Without the seller, sales would certainly drop. This put him in a position to either hold off the sale until he changed his day-to-day impact on the business, or plan on being a contract worker for a buyer in a time frame that would satisfy the buyer of a smooth transition and full takeover. Not exactly a retirement the seller had planned.

He had some choices to make. But the lesson learned is that the value of a business is in the eye of the beholder. In this case, that would be a potential buyer. For top dollar, a seller must think like a buyer and start preparing the business for sale a good three to five years before it's time to sell, if not right from day one.

Courtesy of George Sierchio, Accredited Business Coach, Seasoned Buy/Sell Intermediary, Speaker, and Author

Action Business Partners, Inc.

P.O. Box 5454

Parsippany, NJ 07054

Phone: 973-394-9800

Email: info@actionbusinesspartners.com

Web: http://actionbusinesspartners.com/

Would your "house" be ready to show?

Let's shift gears for a minute. Think about your house: the place you may have left several hours, unmade beds, and unfinished projects ago. Would it look appealing, smell appealing, feel appealing to a prospective buyer? Would it be the kind of place that someone would want to raise a family, bring friends to, feel comfortable in?

Could it sell itself? Or would you need to do a little explaining, a little blushing about the peeling paint, the leaking faucets, the unkempt lawn, the cracked window, the noisy neighbors? Would you have to make excuses for things? Justify your asking price? Take less than you intended or needed?

Would it "show" better if you had a little time to get it ready? Sure.

Time to fix things up

Jeffrey D. Jones, ASA, CBA, CBI, president of Advanced Business Brokers in Houston, says, "It generally takes, on average, between five to eight months to sell most businesses. Keep in mind that an average is just that. Some businesses will take longer to sell, while others will sell in a shorter period of time."

Many businesses may take up to one year to sell

However, the reality is that many business owners really don't do anything to prepare for the sale until a few weeks or even days before putting it "in play" on the market. They mistakenly think that the business can sell itself, much in the same way that a home is bought merely after a drive-by.

What would a buyer see in a drive-by of your business?

What would his first impressions be of your:

- Parking lot. Is it in poor repair? Are the shrubs overgrown? Do you have enough space for employees, handicapped persons, and visitors? Is there trash on the lot's surface?
- Entrance way. Has it been swept, shoveled? Does it give a neat appearance of your business? Is it easy to find from the parking lot?
- Reception area. Is there one? Is it neat and clean? Are visitors greeted quickly and with courtesy? Who else is in the waiting area?
- Employees. What are they doing? Are they busy, talking, waiting around, drinking coffee? Do they acknowledge the visitor? Are they smiling? Are they neat, clean, well-presented? Are their desks and filing areas neat or cluttered?
- Cosmetic appearance. How is the lighting? Do the walls need paint? Is the carpet worn? Does everything look "dated?"

What would be said about your business?

Photocopy the following information, walk around, and look. Check your parking lot, reception area, your vehicles, and other places that the public sees. What impression do you have? What leaves you with a good feeling? (Score 5) A poor feeling? (Score 1)

ITEM	IMPRESSION	REMARKS
Building signage:	1 2 3 4 5	_____
Parking lot:	1 2 3 4 5	_____
Grounds:	1 2 3 4 5	_____
Vehicles' signage:	1 2 3 4 5	_____
Visual condition of lettered vehicles (they're really traveling billboards!):	1 2 3 4 5	_____
Office reception area:	1 2 3 4 5	_____
Inside work areas:	1 2 3 4 5	_____
Storage areas:	1 2 3 4 5	_____
Shipping/receiving areas:	1 2 3 4 5	_____
Other: _____	1 2 3 4 5	_____
Other: _____	1 2 3 4 5	_____
Other: _____	1 2 3 4 5	_____
Other: _____	1 2 3 4 5	_____

TO-DO LIST OF IMPROVEMENTS

1 _____   5 _____
2 _____   6 _____
3 _____   7 _____
4 _____   8 _____

Make them drool

Sophisticated sellers know what buyers are looking for and try to enhance their business by molding it to appeal to buyers. In simplest terms, buyers want to see a business that is well run, well managed, well stocked, with employees who are productive, motivated, and happy. (It doesn't hurt if they're clean, flexible, and loyal – these are nice perks to sweeten the deal!)

Your job, as the business owner, is to make the buyer drool over your business. So, you'll want to do everything possible to make sure that you can come as close to creating that ideal "dream house" that the buyer is looking to purchase. To do this, you will have to address the following key elements:

- Appearance
- Documentation
- Employees
- Liabilities
- Assets
- Contracts
- Reputation
- Financial Statements

Appearance should not be deceiving

The cliché about lasting first impressions getting no second chances are certainly applicable to the selling of your business. If it doesn't look good, most buyers will, in essence, just "drive by." This isn't to suggest that you need to go out and hire an interior decorator for your reception area, but you should make sure that it gets a good scrubbing behind the ears. People equate sloppy appearance with sloppy practices. Therefore, you need to make sure that the buyer sees an environment and a work force that is reflective of the image you have in the community and the industry. If you're selling a "fast, focused, and flexible" future to your buyer, then make sure that your business appears to parallel your goals.

What do you need to change (regarding physical appearances)?

In addition to those items on your "walk-around list" from an earlier page, there may be other changes you need to make in the physical appearance of your company. List those changes here, or fire up the word processor and make your own list:

1. _____ 6. _____

2. _____ 7. _____

3. _____ 8. _____

4. _____ 9. _____

5. _____ 10. _____

Documentation: Creating a Management Book

Buyers like evidence. Sure, they "want" to believe you, but you'll build a much stronger case if you have actual printed proof of the initiatives and agenda you say you have in place. Today's buyers are very sophisticated, bringing with them business degrees from major universities and the inherent need to see and process data. They like to see paper, read numbers, and carry away documents that say – at least to them – that your business is the well-managed operation that you say it is.

Therefore, a Management Book needs to be prepared. Some professionals may have other names for this document, such as Selling Memorandum or Selling Prospectus. Regardless of what it is called, this document will be the package used to market your company to qualified buyers. And it needs to have a professional appearance. Your engaged intermediary can assemble it – with your help and input, of course. It needs to contain sections that discuss, at a minimum:

Company History (including Mission Statement)

Finance
- Corporate Structure (C-Corporation, S-Corporation, LLC, etc.)
- Stockholder/Member Names, Percentage of Ownership, and Agreements
- Financial Statements
- Explanation of Adjusted Earnings, including Add-backs
- Accounting Practices, including Outstanding A/R and A/P
- Budget Documents (including Allowances for Damages, Refunds, and Returns)
- Leases

Human Resources
- Organizational Chart
- Key Management Personnel Bio-Sketches
- List of All Job Descriptions
- Recruiting and Training Practices
- Personnel Policy Manual/Handbook (outline)
- Professional Certifications (if applicable)
- Work Schedules
- Employment Contracts
- Union Contracts

Operations Division and/or Service Department (including Mission Statements for each)
- Product or Service Lines (descriptions)
- Production Reports (include samples)
- Operations Manuals (descriptions or outlines only)
- Quality Control Practices (descriptions or outlines only)
- Backlogs

Material Control
- Inventory Management Practices
- Suppliers and Vendors

Research and Development Practices

Engineering, Repair and Maintenance
- Physical Plant Facilities (describe)
- Equipment (production and computer – describe)
- Repair and Maintenance Practices

Information Technology (IT)/Management Information Services
- Computerization Practices (describe software)

Sales, Marketing, Public Relations, Customer Service
- Description of Market Area
- Description of Competition
- Market Share
- Sales Trends
- Public Relations Practices
- Customer Service Practices

Status of any Audits, Investigations, or Litigation
> Government Audits (i.e. IRS, State Tax, Workers Compensation, etc.)
> Regulatory/Licensing Audits
> EPA Issues

Antitrust Issues

Other
> Include anything else you feel presents the current nature of your company.

The benefits of a Management Book, from the buyer's point of view, are two-fold. First, they offer proof that the decisions made in your business are based on a solid foundation; and secondly, they give the buyer some tangible tools to use in continuing to run the business after the sale.

If you don't have these things in place, get busy. The creation of items such as organizational charts and operation manuals may seem like a waste of production time to you, but buyers view these as evidence of a well-managed and well-run company, having a value that a buyer will pay for. This is because you have offered proof of what you professed, and therefore lessened the risk factor of the sales transaction.

Anything that you can do to develop and document systems and standard operating procedures will definitely enhance the salability of your business. The new owner needs to feel confident that the business can run successfully without you.

When putting together a Management Book, keep in mind the cliche that "honesty is the best policy." Later on in the sale process, an activity known as "due diligence" will come into play. During due diligence, a savvy buyer will employ a team of professional experts to verify, document, and audit all of the information that appears in your Management Book.

Employees

Most buyers dislike change. They are buying your business for an investment, not as a career. Therefore, they will want to retain those employees who are integral to the continuing success of the business. A buyer's worst fear is that the day he takes over the company, you and your crew will jump ship. A way to alleviate this fear – and reduce the risk factor for the buyer – is to first identify the key employees and then offer bonuses to them, tying them into an agreement to remain with the company for a specified period of time. However, this is something to negotiate with the buyer – as he will probably be agreeable to the bonus idea, but perhaps not to the bonus recipients.

The buyer will want to hear your recommendations, so be sure to have updated performance reviews and resumes of your key players on hand to support your case.

Liabilities

A buyer doesn't want to inherit your debts. If he is expected to do so, you can expect to receive a lower price for your company. So, make sure that your house is in order and free from as many contingent liabilities as possible before you approach a potential buyer.

Settle all legal disputes before closing the deal, or you will have to adjust the selling price. The same is true for any disagreements you have with vendors, suppliers, or customers. Remember that your goal is to present your company as being well-managed, so do what you can – ahead of time – to remedy any legal or communication difficulties you may have.

And, don't forget the IRS. If you sell the business with unresolved tax claims, the IRS can put a tax lien against your property – at just about the same time you want to make your deal. This could take the most opportune moment and make it vanish – much in the same way that unresolved pension claims or insurance claims could. Taxing entities have earned a reputation for dragging their feet – possibly just long enough for the buyer to find time to walk away from what could have been the "perfect" deal.

A labor union could be another liability for the buyer – if the timing of the sale is not properly planned. A buyer will not want to buy your company when a union contract is about to expire or is being negotiated. So, if possible, sell your company in the first year of a union contract.

Remember – you want a smooth sale.

Assets

Buyers want to know what they are getting for their money. Take a physical count of your company's inventory and its equipment. You might be surprised to see that there is a significant difference between what you have on your books versus what you have in your warehouse. The buyer wants to know the actual count. He will want:

- A list of inventory
- Cost invoices
- Physical count of equipment
- Physical count of inventory
- Physical count of supplies

For certain capital equipment, you may need to engage the services of a professional appraiser to document actual values. If real estate is included as a part of what you are offering for sale, you may need to have it appraised by a competent professional.

Again, more proof equals less risk.

Contracts

You will need to look at the various contracts you have and determine if they will be transferable to the new buyer. These will include loans (if the buyer is assuming your debt) and contracts concerning any professional services (office cleaning, office supplies, copy machine maintenance, etc.), customer or client awarded contracts – and, most specifically, real estate leases.

In the case of a retail operation – or any business where success depends on location – a favorable lease is essential for a favorable sale. The lease is also a key element to consider for a business that can be relocated without serious damage, but with significant costs. A buyer will look at the expense and difficulty of a move and place a lower value on the business accordingly. Even a relatively easy and seemingly inexpensive move will be a negative concern to a lot of buyers who want to see a minimal amount of change in the early stages of ownership. Often, the last thing a new owner wants to do is move the business he or she just bought.

The good news is that most leases – and contracts – are transferable.

If you are doing your homework and taking the necessary time to get your house in order, then you can talk to your landlord and negotiate a transferable lease if you don't currently have one. You can also take this approach with the various suppliers, clients, and customers that are currently partnered with your business in some type of contract. Most businesses – yours as well as theirs – thrive on continuity. So be upfront about your plans and your desires in order to maintain a risk-free transaction to all parties involved.

Reputation

You can run but you can't hide. If you've been a "bad boy" when running your business, the prospective buyer will find out. A buyer will check out both your personal reputation and the reputation of your company. He will dig into the darkest corners of where you live, where you work, and where you stand in the industry and in your community. He will ask a lot of questions – by interviewing a lot of people. And he'll probably check your credit through the three major credit reporting bureaus.

Buyers will want to hear glowing reviews about you and the company you keep. They will want to hear that you are honest and reliable, and that your company sells quality products or services at a fair price within a consistent and timely manner.

So if you have a skeleton – even if it's way, way back there – see what you can do to dust it off and make it shine, along with your reputation.

Financial Statements

Of all things that a buyer looks at, the financial statements of your business will be the one most scrutinized, examined, and dissected. With expert precision – and with the help of expert advisors using the latest computer technology and software – the prospective buyer will be looking for proof that your business is profitable. He will do this by reviewing your financial statements – for the most recent month, and going back as far as three or more years.

These statements will be used to compare your business with similar businesses in your industry. Yes, the buyer has access to such information.

However, that's probably not what your financial statements have been used for in the past. Many small and mid-size companies summarize their financial performance for tax purposes only. And, since companies are taxed on profits, your past returns may have been prepared to show your company's profits to be as low as legally permissible under state and federal tax codes.

Thus, the buyer will want you – or, more precisely, your accountant – to adjust your statements so they show a more accurate picture of the earning potential of your business. This is known as "recasting" your financial statements.

With these in hand, the buyer can examine trends such as sudden decreases or increases. He will also look at sales activities in terms of product line, customer base, and monthly and quarterly performance.

In addition to profits, the buyer will also be looking at your inventory and your accounts receivable.

Obsolete inventory is of no value to the buyer. Neither are receivables more than 90-days old. Both categories will be used against you in terms of your asking price. Sell the old inventory and equipment, and take the bad receivables with you and write them off.

Also, consider anything personal that you or your family has been receiving as perks. These would include all non-operating items of a personal nature – cars; motor homes; boats; airplanes; gasoline and other credit cards; the corporate "retreat" (read: the summer vacation home!); family-owned real estate that is rented or leased back to the corporation at higher-than-market-value rates – anything that doesn't contribute to sales. When your accountant recasts your financial statements, the costs of these items drop to the bottom line as increased profits, which can increase the price you receive from a buyer.

As you review your financial statements for recasting, you also need to consider any legitimate, one-time extraordinary expenses that may have affected your profitability in recent years. Perhaps your company suffered a major loss not covered by insurance; you had to resist a unionization attempt; you were required to pay for an environmental cleanup project. While each of these items was costly – and adversely affected your profits in a given year – it is likely that they are one-time-only events and will not recur. Such items need to be considered during the recasting process.

Any items that increase the bottom line after recasting your financial statements are known as "add-backs." It is in your best interest to calculate (and explain with footnotes) all of the add-backs before submitting your recast financials to a potential buyer. In most cases, the add-backs will show increased profitability that, in turn, makes your company more valuable, especially if it is priced on a "multiple-of-earnings" basis.

No wonder it takes a year!

If you're like most business owners, you realize that there is a little more work to selling your business than you may have realized – at least if your goal is to sell the business for a price that is satisfying, or even delightful.

But that's why you've called in some helpers. The lawyer, accountant, and intermediary will assist you in their various areas throughout the process to make sure that you are presenting your business in the most favorable, honest, and salable light possible.

Creating Your Preliminary Prospectus

Does your business have some type of advertising piece or sales slick or brochure used to entice customers to buy your product or service? A website? Certainly. The days of "word-of-mouth" advertising are virtually nonexistent. So are the days of word-of-mouth business sales.

For the same reasons that you possess printed and online materials to entice prospective customers or clients to do business with you, you need similar tools to entice prospective buyers to look at your company when it's for sale.

As you've read earlier, the potential buyers of your business will be smart, savvy, and sophisticated. They are busy, interested in a smooth transaction, and probably looking at your company as well as several others. They demand information, but don't have time to dig for it. They will be impressed by your ability to present your company in a well-thought-out, well-documented package – offering answers to their questions about its performance, people and plans.

One recommended way to do this is to prepare a sales tool for your company. Your intermediary is experienced and skilled at putting together such a package. A Preliminary Prospectus is a document the buyer can review before receiving a copy of your Management Book. It needs to include the following sections:

- Sales Pitch
- Photographs/Video on CD (optional)
- Company History
- Selling Price and Terms
- Company External Environment
- Employee Information
- Asset Assessment
- Environmental Issues
- Client List (generic)
- Outstanding Contracts or Agreements
- Location(s) Description(s)

- Plans for the Future
- Supporting Financial Documentation
- Product or Service Literature

Sales Pitch

Blow your own horn. This is your chance to really sell the business. Use the same techniques, terminology, and excitement found in a brochure for your product or service. Emphasize what's great about the business, why the buyer should snatch it. Focus on growth potential and climate, and make the buyer want to hear more.

Photographs/Video/PowerPoint on CD

You way want to whet the buyer's appetite by including one page of color photographs, or a PowerPoint presentation, or a short video presentation of the outside of your main office location; of additional locations; of company vehicles; or of your finished product coming off a production line.

This is not absolutely necessary, but such a presentation would tend to give the buyer a visual perspective of your business.

Company History

In this section, you will need to give a complete description of your company. This includes your products and services, your markets, and your industry profile. This will also include your real reasons for wanting to sell the business. In this section, the buyer is looking to form some type of historical profile of your company as well as project it into the future. So, you will want to include your plans for the future development and growth of the business – even if they are just visions and not clearly substantiated business objectives.

In all areas of the document – but especially in this one – you need to exercise your honesty and integrity. List your company's strengths and weaknesses, detail the areas where you've done a great job, and highlight those where improvements can and should be made. Again, this will show that your company is managed through a systematic process that has taken it through the years of its success.

In selling your company to the strategic buyer, you will want to emphasize all the opportunities for growth that existed, but that you could not take advantage of because of your lack of key personnel or lack of capital. You can include things about your plans to open new marketing channels, requests for bids in certain areas, etc.

Selling Price and Terms

In this area, you want to weed out tire kickers, but whet the appetite of those really interested and able to pay for your company. In other words, you want to be general, yet specific.

You might include something like this:

"This is a restricted private offering of the negotiated sale of ABC Corporation of Brooklyn, New York. All inquiries concerning this offering need to be directed to (name and address of your intermediary), the exclusive agent to the sale. All shares of the company are offered for a price to be negotiated, payable in cash at closing. The offer will be withdrawn after January 1, ———."

You don't need to say anything more about the price or terms at this point. You have presented the basic terms as well as established the tone of the sale.

Company External Environment

Obtain as much market research data about your business and about your industry as possible – especially if it supports the future growth of your company. Project into a three- to five-year future target.

Sometimes the information you seek isn't readily available. However, be aware the buyer will be asking you to prove the size and growth of your industry, and the key customers who have helped you in the past and will probably be around during the company's foreseeable future.

Begin your data search with credit reports on competitors. These will help you build and prove the industry average. List the competitor's name, revenue, and profits. If you have data from past years, you can begin to see a trend and formulate an average of those profit growths. How do they compare with your business?

A buyer wants to know how this business stacks up against the rest – even if it isn't favorable. By presenting a true picture of the market share that your business enjoys, the buyer can identify what areas to target as well as what competitors to follow.

With all data, be aware that numbers generated through third party sources will be viewed as more credible than those coming from your accounting or marketing folks.

Employee Information

The greatest fear of any buyer is that key employees will leave the company once ownership has changed.

In this section of your documentation, you need to discuss all the employees within your organization – and sell the buyer on what a great bunch of people they (truly) are. You need to describe the number of hourly or commissioned employees, whether (or not) they are represented by a union, their job titles, pay rates, and number of years employed.

Your management team is of special interest to the buyer, who will be looking at these individuals very closely.

Other than including an organizational chart of all salaried employees, you will also need to include some more tangible information about each member of your management team. At a minimum, this information includes the employee's:

Function

Title

Name (optional)

Years of service

Annual salary

Number of direct reports

Date of expiration of employment agreement

Key managers need to have some more detailed information attached to their brief bios. This would include their educational background, experience with your company, and the accomplishments critical to the past and future success of your business.

If you have identified a person to run the company when you're gone, devote as much space as necessary to present a complete and glowing description of this individual. If you will be running the business for the new owner, dazzle him with your descriptive resume and accomplishments related to your company's success.

Asset Assessment

In this section, you will discuss the real estate, leases (and expiration dates), machinery, equipment, furniture, fixtures, and other capital items associated with the business. The buyer will need details on which of these you plan to sell, keep personally, or leave behind and include in the asking price so that no misunderstanding will occur.

For all assets, you will need to list them with the fair market value. In essence, this tells the buyer that you understand the worth of these things. But to lessen any suspicion that the buyer may have with your estimates, refrain from using the book value on these products – and document your reasoning. As mentioned earlier, the services of a professional appraiser may help with this effort.

In organizing this section of the document, you can include a brief summary of your assets and your intended actions regarding their disposition after the sale. In an appendix, however, you will need to line-item each asset and its age – and explain if it is owned, leased, or being financed (and if financed, the balance owed and to whom).

Environmental Issues

Regardless of the type of industry in which your company operates, all buyers today are highly sensitive to issues that may pose any threat of an environmental hazard. The manner in which your company routinely disposes of the contents of office waste baskets is of concern to buyers. This concern is compounded if you store or use chemicals in any phase of your operation, if you deal with medical patients, or if you maintain vehicles or machinery within your walls.

In this section, you need to address any possible issue that may involve contamination of the environment. Tell how chemicals are stored and the method you use to dispose of them. If there are storage tanks on your property, disclose their number, sizes, registration, and licensing requirements. If storage tanks have been removed, mention their number, sizes, when and how they were removed, and what remedial action took place. If your property recently underwent an environmental audit – perhaps in connection with a bank loan – mention the outcome of the audit.

Generic Client List

A buyer is concerned how a change of your company's ownership may affect your customer or client base – especially those customers or clients who generate a minimum of eight percent of your annual sales. Will these customers change their loyalty to the company when it's sold? Or will there be no change in their buying habits? Answers to these questions can affect the price a buyer is willing to pay for your company.

In this section, include a generic list of major clients – those who each generate a minimum of eight percent of your annual sales – along with either the annual dollar sales volume or percentage of total sales generated from each source, and the length of time they have been buying from your company at the current purchasing level. Since this information is proprietary and highly confidential, it is best not to list the customer's name. A generic name, such as "Customer A" or "Client B," will serve to show the buyer the information he needs for now. Later, during the due diligence phase of the transaction, you will be obligated to make a full disclosure of all customer and client information.

Contracts and Agreements

The buyer will need to know the nature, terms, and conditions of all outstanding contracts and agreements to which your company is a party. This includes such items as union contracts, pension plan contributions, insurance, advertising, dealership, buying and licensing agreements, franchising agreements, and contracts covering trash hauling and building/grounds maintenance.

Make an all-inclusive list, along with expiration dates of each agreement.

Location

It is probable that you won't be selling your business to the guy down the street. It's even possible that the buyer won't be in your town or your state. That's why it's necessary to sell the location of your business. You can obtain a current picture of the location land and the surrounding community by contacting your local Chamber of Commerce or local community development commission. They have slick brochures and information packets designed to do this job for you. So, use them to enhance this section of your document.

Projections

This section need not be long nor disclose any company secrets. As a good rule, limit your discussion to three long-term goals that can be substantiated with marketing or industry-related facts. These goals should already have come up in your discussions about Company History.

Besides telling the buyer what you'd like to do, also list some strategies for accomplishing these things in general. If one of your goals is to introduce a new product, your strategy is that you have a plan for development and marketing.

Remember, he is not buying yet. Whet the appetite – don't drown the deal!

Supporting Financial Documentation

The financial section of your document is the one that will be most closely read, debated upon, and scrutinized. It needs to contain the following components:

1. Three years of financial statements. This would mean your company's balance sheets, income statements, and cash flow statements. These should be recast to show the true nature of your common profitability – as compared

to the lack of profitability, as often portrayed to the Internal Revenue Service.

2. A true identification of how much money you have taken out of the business in the past (the add-backs) and how much you plan to take out in the future, if the business is not sold.

This section does not require full details. Those will come as the deal progresses.

There are two schools of thought regarding the inclusion of a pro forma financial statement in this section. One school says, "Do it. Sell the future. Show the buyer what this business is capable of doing." The other school says, "No, don't include a pro forma. A savvy buyer will develop his own pro forma. Anyhow, a buyer is going to operate the business in the way he sees fit, regardless of what your pro forma says." Besides, as the seller, you don't want to be placed in the position of having your pro forma included as an item in the "warranties and guarantees" section of the final agreement.

Product and Service Literature

In this section, include any business literature, brochures, fliers, menus, CDs, DVDs, etc. that you use to sell your product or service to your customers or clients.

Caution!

Confidentiality is important when preparing your Preliminary Prospectus. Refrain from including anything in this document that could hurt your business. In other words – even though the prospective buyer has signed a Confidentiality Agreement – prepare the report as if a competitor were going to read it.

Summary information checklist

What follows is a checklist of items that will be needed for the preparation of a comprehensive plan to sell your company. These items may or may not be disclosed to a buyer. They are used to answer specific questions that the buyer may raise, and they are helpful to the intermediary during the negotiation process.

FINANCIAL STATEMENTS

- ___ Annual statements for relevant period immediately prior to valuation date, minimum of three years
- ___ Federal income tax returns for the same years (Form 1120 only)
- ___ Most-current monthly financial statement

OTHER FINANCIAL SCHEDULES

- ___ Aged accounts receivable list
- ___ Aged accounts payable list
- ___ List of loans to and from officers, directors, and stockholders
- ___ Depreciation schedules, including real estate and equipment lists, date of acquisition, cost, depreciation method and life, and net depreciated value
- ___ Inventory list
- ___ Officers' and directors' compensation schedule, including all employee benefits and expenses allowed
- ___ Stockholders list and agreements

MISCELLANEOUS FINANCIAL INFORMATION

- ___ Schedule of key-person life insurance

___ Available budgets or projections
___ Capital expense requirements
___ Order backlog (total dollars)
___ Customer base (list of largest customers with amount of sales to each in past year)
___ Supplier list (list of largest suppliers with amount of purchases from each in past year)

EVIDENCE OF REAL AND PERSONAL PROPERTY VALUES
___ Copies of any independent appraisal reports

COPIES OF CONTRACTUAL OBLIGATIONS
___ Including, but not limited to, such items as leases, loan guarantees, franchise or distribution agreements, contracts with customers and/or suppliers, buy/sell agreements, ESOP (Employee Stock Ownership Plan) documentation, employment or non-compete agreements, and union contracts (if applicable).
___ Information regarding any "off balance sheet" assets or liabilities

CORPORATE RECORDS
___ Articles of incorporation and bylaws (or articles of partnership, or LLC operating agreements, as applicable)
___ Minutes book

MISCELLANEOUS INFORMATION
___ Company history
___ Product or service brochures, catalogs, price lists

___ List of key personnel, with position title, tenure, and biographical data

___ List of patents and copyrights

___ List of trade association memberships and industry information sources

___ Business plan (if any)

___ Description of computers, software, and EDP department information

___ Hours of operation

___ Employee mix and work schedules

___ EPA issues

___ Status of all litigation issues

___ Names, addresses, and phone numbers of all outside advisors (attorney, accountant, financial planner)

Perspective of a contributing writer...

REQUIRED INFORMATION
By Scott D. Mashuda, CBI

The specific information that will be required by a business broker or intermediary to prepare your business for sale depends upon the industry in which your business operates. However, certain information will be necessary and beneficial regardless of industry:

- Three to Five Years Historical Financial Statements/ Tax Returns. Although a business buyer will be paying you for what the business is set to accomplish going forward (as of the

date of sale), he will look to your historical financial statements (and tax returns) to assess the risk of your anticipated earnings stream.
- Interim Financial Statements for the last Three Fiscal Periods. Very few business transactions will close at the end of a company's fiscal year. As a result, interim financial statements will be required by a buyer and your intermediary to fill the void between the company's most recent fiscal year end statements and the current date/date of sale.
- List of Assets Included and Excluded in the Sale. Your intermediary will need to demonstrate to a buyer exactly what he is getting in return for his investment. Having a prepared list of both tangible and intangible assets included and excluded from the transaction not only helps clearly present to a buyer what he is getting, but also helps eliminate any discrepancies at closing.
- Schedule of Indebtedness of the Business. Whether the proposed transaction is an "asset sale" or a "stock sale" will determine the relevancy of this information. If only the assets are being purchased by the acquirer, the existing debt obligations will remain the responsibility of the seller and be of interest to the buyer only to make certain that all claims to the assets are removed at closing. However, if the buyer is purchasing an equity stake in the company, he will need to understand the company's full financial picture in order to make a buying decision.
- Prior Appraisal and Valuation Reports. Although a current valuation or appraisal may

be one of the services offered by, or provided through, your intermediary, providing previously completed valuation reports will help your professionals and buyers understand how your business has changed and grown over time.

- Business Plans and Projections. Although a buyer will look to the historical financial statements for an understanding of risk, price will be determined based on what the business is set up to achieve going forward as of the date of sale. Nobody has a better understanding of this than you, the seller. The best way to demonstrate your future expectations is to prepare a business plan that includes financial projections.
- Marketing Materials. Nobody knows your business and its products or services better than you do. Chances are you've been selling the benefits of your products and services to customers for years. There's no need for your representatives to re-create the wheel. The benefits of your products and services to your customers are the same ones your intermediary will need to sell to a prospective purchaser.
- Economic and Industry Data. Although your intermediary will do his own economic and industry research, there may be information available to you as an industry insider that is not readily available through external sources. Providing this information to your intermediary will help him cast your business in the best possible light when working with buyers.
- Copy of any Company Lease Obligations. Similar to the schedules of indebtedness, these

are most relevant when assumed by a buyer. However, even in an asset sale, buyers will want to know that no third party claims exist to the purchased assets.

- Organizational Chart. There is a difference between ownership and management. Although the sale of your business will result in a change of ownership, most buyers will not want to see a change in management. The skills and expertise of your work force and management are one of the things attracting the buyer to your business. An organizational chart will provide a new owner with a clear picture of identified roles and responsibilities.

- Copies and Descriptions of Patents, Trademarks, Trade Names, Existing Research and Development, and Other Intellectual Property. Although the majority of this information will not be fully disclosed or revealed until the due diligence phase, having this information prepared in advance will allow for a more timely process and help to attract a diverse group of buyers.

- Stockholder Agreements. Similar to the schedule of indebtedness and lease obligations, stockholder agreements are most important to a buyer considering an ownership stake in the existing company. However, even a buyer purchasing the assets will want to know that no outside entities have a claim to these assets.

- List of Competitors. Providing a list of competitors to your intermediary will not only help ensure that the proper precautions are taken to maintain confidentiality, but it may also provide a starting point for uncovering potential acquirers.

Not all of this information may be readily available or necessary to complete your transaction. However, the more information that you can provide to your intermediary about your business, the better job they can do in marketing your business. The result of your hard work will be more buyers brought to the table by your broker/intermediary, all competing for your business.

Courtesy of Scott D. Mashuda,
Certified Business Intermediary (CBI)
River's Edge Alliance Group, LLC
PO Box 24553
Pittsburgh, PA 15234
Phone: 412-894-3244
E-mail: smashuda@RiversEdgeAlliance.com
Web: http://www.RiversEdgeAlliance.com/

CHAPTER FIVE

Finding the Right Buyer for Your Business

Finding the Right Buyer for Your Business

Whom would you pick to buy your business?

Without reading further and without consulting anything but your own head and your own gut, whom would you pick to buy your business? Take out a piece of paper and write down the name(s). Following each name, write down the reason(s) why.

You may be right.

But, then again, you may be thinking too locally. Many business owners think that their best bet for a fair sale and a quick transaction will come through selling the business to a company in their own market area – often to a competitor. In fact, selling to the competition is more than likely the response you listed above. At first glance, selling to a competitor makes sense. They know your industry and they probably know your company.

However, you will want to entice as many prospects to your business as possible – and competitors represent just one category.

Other potential buyers include:

- Customers
- Suppliers
- Employees

- Individual Investors
- Larger Diversified Companies
- Private Equity Groups
- Industry Consolidators

Weeding through these prospects is the job of your intermediary. However, you as the final decision maker need to be aware of some of the pros and cons associated with selling your business to each of these groups.

Selling to a competitor

Even though it seems like the logical first choice, many business owners are reluctant to pursue this route because they don't want the competition to tell everyone that the business is for sale. In a business owner's mind, the leak of this secret will create rumors that could lead to a loss of business and loyalty. This is probably not as certain as the business owner imagines. However, it's hard to alter competitive relationships – especially when financial and private matters will now be out in the open.

Another reason for the reluctance to sell to the competition is a business owner's feeling that "everyone is doing better than we are." In many cases, this is more perception than truth.

However, your biggest risk for selling to a competitor occurs if the deal falls through. If this happens, the competitor knows all of your secrets. This information could give him the advantage needed to challenge you in the marketplace. He may now know enough to actually destroy your business.

Be aware that many competitors are "tire kickers." They view the opportunity to buy your company as nothing more than an exploratory fact-finding mission. The difficulties lie in figuring out a competitor's true intentions.

Therefore, consider selling to a competitor only after all other qualified buyers have dropped from the race.

Customers or suppliers

Basically, the same advice offered about competitors is true for customers and suppliers. If you've already forgotten what that is, reread the section above, "Selling to a competitor."

Could employees be buyers?

Certainly. The IRS even encourages it. There are several reasons why employee buyouts make sense:
- It will generate goodwill in the work force.
- You'll definitely be viewed as a good guy.
- You'll be entitled to some healthy tax benefits.

However, don't rush out and put a FOR SALE notice on the employee bulletin board just yet.

Because employees usually don't have enough money to pay cash for your company, employee buyouts are subject to certain risks. The biggest of these is the deal falling through if the employees can't agree to the purchase price or the terms. If the deal fails, you will probably encounter a strained relationship between yourself and the work force. Some employees may leave. Others won't trust you. If you end up selling to an outsider, many employees will treat the new owner poorly, because they may be convinced that the employees should be the "real" owners.

Employees will also want you to sell the company at a reduced price. They may also request other concessions, and more time to come up with the funds. They will literally "know your business," because all aspects concerning your financial profile will be available during negotiations.

Even the most loyal employees can become greedy, envious, or angry. If the deal is successful, but the business is not, the employees will blame you – and in the worst-case scenario, take you to court for a fraudulent conveyance action.

Isn't anyone qualified to buy?
Individual investors represent another buying group. Trends show that former middle managers and senior level executives often court the idea of buying their own business to run. However, these buyers are generally without experience in buying businesses or sufficient capital.

Individual investors are cautious. They simply can't afford to offer a high price and thus leave nothing to put into the business to make it grow. As a result, they will not pay for the future growth of your company, but instead base their offer on your company's past performance.

Investor Groups
There are investor groups, sometimes known as Private Equity Groups, or something similar. In these cases, individuals pool their money and put one or two key members in charge of making investments on behalf of the group. Some of these groups look for a business that can benefit (financially) from a synergistic relationship with other companies that they may own.

Investors associated with these groups are usually looking for profitable companies with more than 10 million dollars in annual sales revenue. These groups are money motivated and money conscious. They will look at many businesses before signing on the line.

Strength in size and numbers

Larger companies, whether privately or publicly held, often have the resources to pay your price, and the credit sources available to make the transaction painless.

It is not unusual for one business to be sold to another business, especially if they are in related industries or have similar processes and systems in place. If another company wants to enter your industry, expect a large premium. This is a key buyer to solicit because he wants to enter and become established in your market.

And, if the deal falls through, the risk is minimal. The buyer is not a competitor or in your industry.

Industry Consolidators

"Consolidators" are experienced financial individuals who specialize in acquiring companies in a fragmented industry. They recognize certain synergistic benefits will result when several companies are merged into a larger enterprise.

Depending upon the state of affairs within your industry, you may be able to sell your company, or merge it, during an industry consolidation (sometimes called a "roll-up").

Industries ripe for consolidation typically exhibit certain basic traits. One is a proliferation of primarily local competitors, sometimes called "mom and pop" operations because of their size or single location. Other characteristics include a limited number of strong regional companies with excellent management and an absence of many large, national players. Another distinction is the maintenance of relatively high earnings ratios (profit margins) by companies in the industry. If your industry possesses these characteristics, it may be a textbook case of a fragmented industry that is ready for consolidation.

You may benefit from participating in a roll-up. Your success will be affected by timing – "being in the right place at the right time" – because such activity in an industry tends to follow approximately three-year cycles. (This issue was discussed earlier. If participation in a consolidation or roll-up interests you, refer to Chapter 3, under the section headed, "What's happening outside your doors?")

In search of the right buyer

First of all, this doesn't have to be your job. If you've hired an intermediary, he is already under contract to find potential buyers and bring them to you. A good intermediary has contacts worldwide and access to databases of qualified business buyers.

In confidence

This issue was discussed in an earlier chapter, but it needs to be repeated: Insist that each prospective buyer sign a Confidentiality Agreement. This states that the potential buyer agrees to keep the information about your company confidential and will only use it for evaluation purposes. Although this is not a total guarantee, it does offer some protection for you and your business.

If a prospect will not sign such an agreement, do not give out any information. Such a refusal is all but an admission that this buyer is more interested in fishing for data, not in landing a sale.

Perspective of a contributing writer...

WHO IS THE BUYER FOR YOUR BUSINESS?

By Scott D. Mashuda, CBI

While you may not currently know the answer to this question, understanding the different types of buyers (and their motivations) allows you the ability to position your business in a way that makes it most attractive to the broadest audience.

- Individual Buyers. Individual business buyers are individual people just like you and me. This person will typically only purchase one business in his lifetime. He or she is looking for independence and freedom. He wants to create personal wealth and/or develop a legacy for his family. An individual buyer understands that with business ownership there are sacrifices, both personal and financial. But, these sacrifices are worth it to him (within reason) to obtain freedom of thought, schedule, and decision. The most important characteristics of business targets for individual buyers are location (proximity to their homes and their families), stability, and track record. Most individual buyers have significant experience in the work force and have developed some level of success there. While they are looking for freedom and independence, they are also looking to maintain their current standard of living. Earnings history, a proven track record, and stability are extremely important.

- Strategic Buyers. Strategic buyers include public and private companies both foreign and domestic. These buyers already own and operate existing businesses and are looking to grow or vertically integrate their operations. Attractive acquisitions will allow these companies to diversify their product base, expand their market reach, acquire intellectual property, shorten their research and development cycle, or achieve cost savings. The most important characteristics to this group are size, market share, reputation, developed technology, trademarks, patents, trade names, a skilled work force, and recognizable quality products and/or service. These buyers are looking to grow their companies and expand their corporate footprints by means of acquisition.
- Financial Buyers. Financial buyers include angel investors, private equity firms, and investment funds. These buyers are looking to acquire existing companies with the potential for substantial growth. While the acquisition target may lack a sophisticated management team and capital for growth, these buyers typically bring such resources to the table. They are professional business buyers with serious capital and sophistication. They are looking to infuse their talents and money into an existing organization, grow it exponentially, and sell it in a relatively short timetable for a significant return. As you may reasonably estimate, these buyers are inundated with acquisition opportunities and afforded the luxury of sifting through candidates before settling on their selection. To make the

grade with this group, you must offer stable yet substantial returns with the opportunity for quick growth and a planned exit.

All three buyer types vary in their desires and their approach. Knowing their motivation allows you to position your business so that it is appealing to the broadest audience.

    Courtesy of Scott D. Mashuda,
    Certified Business Intermediary (CBI)
    River's Edge Alliance Group, LLC
    PO Box 24553
    Pittsburgh, PA 15234
    Phone: 412-894-3244
    E-mail: smashuda@RiversEdgeAlliance.com
    Web: http://www.RiversEdgeAlliance.com/

Perspective of a contributing writer...

MAXIMIZE YOUR COMPANY'S SELLING PRICE

By David Mahmood

With the current credit crunch, you may not realize that the middle market – deals ranging in size from $25 million to $500 million – is booming! The key to a winning transaction, however, is not getting the deal done; it is maximizing the return to you and other selling shareholders. To achieve this success, you must accomplish the following:

- More than one potential acquirer must be at the table. Sellers wish to maximize their return, while buyers desire to purchase a company as inexpensively as possible. A confidential silent auction will maximize your selling price. You need to create competition!

- What you want personally is the determining factor in the type of buyers you should approach. If your plan includes staying and running the business for an additional three to five years, a private equity group makes a good buyer. You receive considerable cash at closing and the opportunity to continue running the business while maintaining a significant amount of equity. Private equity groups have more than $180 billion in available capital to invest, and with less leverage available from banks, they are putting much more equity into deals.

  If you wish to exit your business quickly and maximize your return, a strong strategic buyer makes a good choice. Strategic acquirers, both foreign and domestic, have realized outstanding financial performance in the last several years. They have strong cash reserves and are looking for acquisitions that build on core business competencies or that expand the strengths of their current divisions. They are aggressively buying middle-market businesses because they see great opportunity to grow in this tough economy.

- Consider the effects of economic variables: credit scarcities, interest rates, and inflation. While these factors may be largely out of your control, others aren't. It is critical to present your company in the best light, especially in difficult times. Enhance your odds of getting a good

price by having accurate knowledge of your business' worth, provided by an expert valuator.
- Timing is everything. Now is the time to sell, before the market becomes flooded with troubled companies. Good businesses always sell – they sell better when timed and marketed well.

Courtesy of David Mahmood, Founder and
Chairman, Allegiance Capital Corporation
5429 LBJ Freeway, Suite 750
Dallas, TX 75240
Phone: 214-217-7732
E-mail: dmahmood@allcapcorp.com
Web: http://www.allcapcorp.com/

CHAPTER SIX

Making the Right Deal

Making the Right Deal

What's your worry?

As you read in the last section, a competent intermediary will be responsible for bringing the best buyer to your door. Part of this person's duty is to eliminate "window shoppers" and "tire kickers," and to carefully screen the more serious contenders and bring them – to meet you halfway – to the negotiation table.

But there is still a risk and a worry. There are a lot of people out there – especially among the ranks of first-time buyers – who are basically unrealistic. They have unfounded expectations of what they can afford and where they can get the financing. Even the most credentialed, well-positioned buyers are likely to raise a few questions and a few points on your blood pressure. As a seller, you may have concerns common to other sellers. You may worry that…

- You might not be getting a fair price
- You might not be paid on time
- You might not be paid at all
- The IRS will take all your profits from the sale
- The new owner will run your business right into the ground

With these ideas in mind, you have every right to ask the buyer this question: "Do you have the money to make this deal

happen?" Then watch the reaction. Carefully listen to what he says about these things:
- Willingness to use his own home as collateral
- The speed and ease of getting a small business loan
- Uncertainty or vagueness about where to get financing, or from whom
- Past credit history and experience with banks
- Overconfidence about "Money is not a problem"

What are YOU most worried about? Take out a piece of paper and write it down.

Buyers lose sleep, too

Even if they've done it before, and even if they've come prepared, buyers spend time mulling over possibilities and replaying conversations and scenarios when they are at the brink of making a deal. While you're tossing and turning in your bed or in your head, your buyer is probably going through the same type of mental gymnastics, trying to find solid answers to his concerns.

Perhaps he is wondering...
- Can I really afford to buy this business?
- Where am I going to come up with the money to do this?
- Am I paying too much?
- Is this business really what it's cracked up to be?

Rest assured

The best remedy for assuring a successful deal is to minimize the risks. This can be done by working through a careful and documented sales plan that allows you – as the seller – to establish the price while being flexible with the terms. If you realize that the terms are really what drives (and closes) the sale, you will be further ahead on achieving your long-term goals, regardless if they relate to financial success or just a peaceful night's rest.

The flexibility of the sales terms usually means your willingness to accept multiple forms of payment from the buyer.

To tie into your thoughts about dreaming, consider this. Wouldn't it be great if somebody would pay you 100 percent CASH for your business, right now, without question, clause, or complications? Sure.

But the reality is, you'd wake up sooner or later – probably from the knock on your bank account by the IRS. Furthermore, many buyers do not have the financial resources or the desire to pay for your business entirely in cash. In fact, many of them would like to see you put up all the cash!

In their dreams, right?

That's why most deals happen somewhere in between the fantasies of the buyer and the dreams of the seller. And in many cases, this happy medium is struck through at least partial owner financing. In plain talk – you play the roleof "banker."

You play the banker

Did you ever try to get a loan from a bank? If so, you're all too familiar with how the system works. Seldom is the business alone enough to secure the financing you are requesting. Instead, the bank demands that you offer them collateral (real estate or other tangible assets) that can be sold in case you can't pay off the loan.

The same rules apply if you decide to be the banker for the sale of your business. If the new buyer can't pay his loan to you, then you can take the business back and run it. The "security" in the business has a real value to you – but only a minimal value to an actual banker.

Also, while rates on owner financing vary from institution to institution and from year to year, a rate close to the prime rate – or just a little bit higher – is most typical. This means that the deal will probably be financed at a lower rate than the bank will use when lending to small businesses – but at a higher rate than it will use to pay on a certificate of deposit or savings account.

Typically, you as the seller decide on the minimum price you want for the business. Consider taking anything over that amount in owner financing. This minimizes the risk for you. The most you can lose is the amount received that is higher than your lowest acceptable price.

This type of sale – called an "installment sale" – can be very good for both the buyer and the seller. However, be aware of the risk implications. A buyer will see buying your company as his risk and believe that it's only fair that you see some risk too. In the buyer's mind, if you will not take some of the risk, then perhaps your company's future isn't at all what you said it would be.

The fact is that most business sales include some type of owner financing. One final note. If you are considering such a transaction and have personally guaranteed any bank loans, be certain to require indemnification from the buyer in the event any loan is not paid off.

Taking stock in the buyer's company

If you really are interested in deferring your taxes, the easiest way is to take shares of stock in the buyer's company as payment for your company. If the deal is structured properly, doing so will defer your having to pay capital gains taxes until you actually sell the stock of the company that acquired your company.

This, however, involves more risk. You must remember that by accepting stock as payment, you are trading the investment in your own company for an investment in another company. The risk heightens, not only because of the uncertainties of your buyer's ability to run the business, but also from the fluctuations of the stock market itself – or the variations to come in the industry in which the buyer's stock participates.

Other than the advantage from a tax perspective, your acceptance of stock as payment may mean that leases and other agreements with your business could remain intact unless there are specific conditions stating otherwise.

In most sales of this nature, cash, accounts receivables, property, and other assets become the property of the buyer upon closing. He will also inherit all the liabilities such as accounts payable, short-term debt, and long-term debt. However, you would be responsible for any loans that you have personally guaranteed prior to the time of the sale, unless they can be refinanced by the new owner without your signature.

As you are considering the idea of taking stock in the buyer's company, however, you need to ask some important questions:

Is the buyer's stock marketable?

Can you sell the stock whenever you want to, or are there certain restrictions?

Although stock is a commonly accepted form of payment, you need to be clear about one thing: You may be stuck with a bad stock!

Dealing with differences

It will be a rare instance if you and the buyer absolutely agree on the selling price. However, through negotiations and expert facilitation skills provided by your intermediary or attorney, you will eventually come to a middle ground and a way to counter the price with the terms.

But what if you don't? Occasionally, buyers and sellers never agree on a price. This may be because they view the company's earning potential very differently. A seller may believe that the company is ripe for increased sales in the future and the buyer may not see the capabilities of this, based on the firm's past performance. Additionally, there may be something external at work. Perhaps there is the likelihood of a significant event that would negatively or positively affect the earning potential of the business, such as a competitor moving into the location (negative impact) or a huge pending contract due to come in after the sale (positive).

In either scenario, the buyer and seller will not agree. At this point, they may consider an earn-out. This is a purchase arrangement where a portion of the payment is based on the performance of the business after the deal is closed. An earn-out gives the seller the right to receive additional monies if the company reaches certain sales and profitability goals. An earn-out can also act as an incentive for you – if you plan to stay on with the company as part of the management team. It's an assurance to the buyer that you will do everything possible to make certain the business is run at its most profitable level.

If you plan to take this approach, be certain to insist that the benchmarks for the earn-out can be easily measured.

Call in the experts

Remember a few sections back when you read about the importance of paying for good experts? Well, here is where they are really essential. Your tax, legal, and selling professionals are paid to work out the best deal for you. They are the ones who will collectively work with you to formulate and present the asking price and terms of your sale. Don't go it alone here!

Get into the buyer's head

Even if you've had a previous relationship with the buyer, in this scenario you're on opposite teams. You think the buyer's trying to steal your company and the buyer thinks that you're trying to steal his wallet.

You know your suspicions. The buyer, however, is a little reluctant to believe all you are representing to be true about the rosy future of your business. He may be thinking, "If it's so great, why does he want to sell it so quickly?"

Try to understand these feelings and work through responses and strategies for putting him at ease about these suspicions – even if some of them may be founded.

A common negotiation strategy

As the seller, you control the timing of the sale.

However, be aware of a common practice that occurs during the negotiation process – the strategy for all parties to say they have other offers or other deals waiting in the wings. This may be true. And, then again, it may be a strategy.

If a buyer talks about looking at other deals, don't worry. There's really nothing you can do to prevent this. Even if it is not true, your delay may be all it takes to open that window of opportunity for other prospects.

If there's a spark, make it into a flame by securing a commitment as soon as possible.

Commit in writing

At this point in the process – when both you and the buyer are in basic agreement – you both will need to sign a formal document referred to as a "Letter of Intent" or a "Letter of Understanding."

Many such letters contain, in part, verbiage such as "The completion of this transaction is subject to, among other things, negotiation of a definitive agreement and the completion of customary due diligence."

A Letter is a confirmation of the buyer's serious interest in the sale, the price and terms of the sale, and a specific time frame for closing the deal. It should also state any employment considerations and any non-competition agreements.

Even if a Confidentiality Agreement was already signed, the Letter should include verbiage to prohibit the buyer from disclosing any information about the sale of the business or giving away any of your company's proprietary information or trade secrets.

As the seller, you must realize that once you sign this letter, your negotiating power is minimal. It is usually produced by the buyer at the end of the negotiation process, but before a final purchase agreement is drafted. Once it is signed, the buyer will probably insist that your company is no longer "in play." In other words, it is no longer for sale; it is "off the market," and you agree not to solicit offers from other potential buyers.

This Letter is also your cue to inform other players of your intended transaction. This would include any lenders, stockholders who aren't already aware of what's happening, customers, suppliers, and employees.

Show me the money!

If your deal involves a company with annual sales revenues of less than one million dollars, now is the time to ask the buyer for an "earnest money" deposit. Typically, a seller will ask a buyer to put this money into an escrow account. It serves as a form of insurance and eliminates the less-than-serious buyers. Deals involving larger companies normally do not require such a deposit.

Due diligence

"Due diligence" is the acceptable terminology for activity that takes place between the time the Letter of Intent is signed and the execution of the final Purchase Agreement. During this period, both the buyer and the seller do some final and in-depth digging to make certain the proposed deal is acceptable for all concerned. The buyer will be combing your financials, conducting audits, examining contracts, and looking into every aspect of your business, including checking into your past and future claims.

Among other things, many savvy buyers today employ specialists who conduct environmental audits to assure the status of past or future claims involving environmental cleanup issues. In-ground storage tanks, asbestos, and waste disposal methods are of major concern, even if property is leased. Buyers are also sensitive to potential antitrust issues, and may seek opinions of government regulators before moving forward on certain deals.

But you should be busy too. This is your time to truly investigate this buyer. Obtain answers to these questions:

- Can the buyer really AFFORD to purchase the business?
- How will he come up with the FINANCING?
- What does he REALLY WANT out of this deal?
- How QUICKLY can all of this happen?

Once the process of due diligence is ended, your transaction attorney will meet with the buyer's attorney. And other than duking it out with the small-print legalese, the two of them will formulate the final Purchase Agreement. However, because the buyer's attorney will more than likely prepare the final draft of the Agreement, insist that your attorney work on the body of content most affecting your concerns.

The Agreement to Purchase

Even though you will not be personally responsible for drafting this document, you should be aware of its topical content. One way to do this is to insist that the document be written in an understandable, easy to follow manner. All the wording should be clear to all parties, regardless of their level of sophistication or undergraduate degree.

If you are planning to stay with the company as a consultant, make this type of agreement separately from the Purchase Agreement. An Employment Agreement is a personal services contract. If this contract is buried between the paragraphs of the deal, it can be used as a deal-breaker. Generally, in cases of fraud or misrepresentation, lawyers will look at employment contracts for ways to help the buyer get out of the deal.

K.I.S.S.

You've no doubt heard and probably used the acronym for "Keep it Simple, Stupid." It's true in deal-making as well. The more complex the deal, the more likely it is to fall through. Decide what you want and need up front, and work with your advisors on the sale plans and strategies before calling in the buyers. Then, when it comes to negotiations and all the paperwork that follows, make sure that your wording and your requests are simple, direct, and understandable to everyone involved.

CHAPTER SEVEN

Successfully Closing the Sale... and the Door

Successfully Closing the Sale... and the Door

The moment of truth

The actual closing of the sale of your company will probably take place at an attorney's office – in a large conference room – around a large table. The perimeter of the tabletop, in neat piles, will be covered with stacks of papers ready for your signature. Your attorney and the buyer's attorney will escort you and the buyer to the first stack. They will briefly explain the contents of the stack and point to the lines on the pages that require signatures. You'll then move to the next stack and repeat the process – and to the next stack – until you've walked entirely around the table and signed all of the necessary documents. If you're like most sellers, you'll have writer's cramp when you're done – which will be only slightly alleviated when the buyer hands you a check or wire transfer receipt containing a number with a comma, followed by zeros…in groups of three!

You'll then sigh a breath of relief. It's over. It's done. You've sold the company.

The fastest year in history

Regardless of your motivation for selling your business, the year you decide to do it will probably pass as the fastest, most challenging, most exciting one you've experienced in your business career. However, if you've taken time to really think through your options and spent the necessary money to secure the assistance of deal-making professionals, the journey will end with a positive climax.

So, after reading this book up to this page, if you're ready – really ready – to sell your company, remember these key points:
- Hire the right help.
- Prepare your company for sale.
- Recast your financial statements.
- Decide what you really want – and go for it.
- Be honest at all times.
- Investigate the buyer.
- Be true to yourself.

What's your plan?

After the sale of your company, what do you plan to do – after, of course, entering that healthy deposit in your checkbook? Write it down.

Your personal plan

Remember all the hours and thoughts you spent planning to go into business in the first place? Well, you'll have to apply the same basic strategies to get out of business – or at least out of the business mind-set – to have a smooth transition.

Prepare a personal plan to cover this next phase of your life. Regardless of how small they are, start putting these plans into action – immediately. If you plan to travel, buy the tickets. If you plan to jump into a hobby, buy the supplies. If you plan to consult, print your new business cards and start making a few prospective phone calls.

To be a business owner, you obviously have success traits that point to planning and follow-through. Perhaps you might think that you'd like to spend the rest of your life sitting on the couch and watching old movies. But the fact is, you'd soon be dissatisfied with that agenda.

You will have to decide what "having enough" means to you, when you want to stop, when it's time to move on to something else.

The question, then, is where do you go from here?

- What new phase of your life do you want to enter after you have climbed the mountain and reached the top?
- Do you somehow want to stay involved in the business after it's been sold, working in some capacity with the new owner?
- What are you going to do with all of your money? How many speedboats can you ski behind?

The answers to these questions may lie in the reordering of your personal priorities. Perhaps you want to put money away for retirement, or invest it for more immediate gain. Maybe you want to begin contributing more to society, get involved in politics, nonprofit boards, or charities. Or maybe it's a time to take an in-depth look at your entire life.

The Wheel of Life

One way to do this is to examine what is called the Wheel of Life. This is not a new concept; it's been around for a number of years. It's unclear who is credited with first having developed it.

It essentially involves six elements and how they interact with one another:

- Physical Health
- Relationships and Family Life

- Ethical and Spiritual Concerns
- Mental Attitude
- Financial
- Social Life

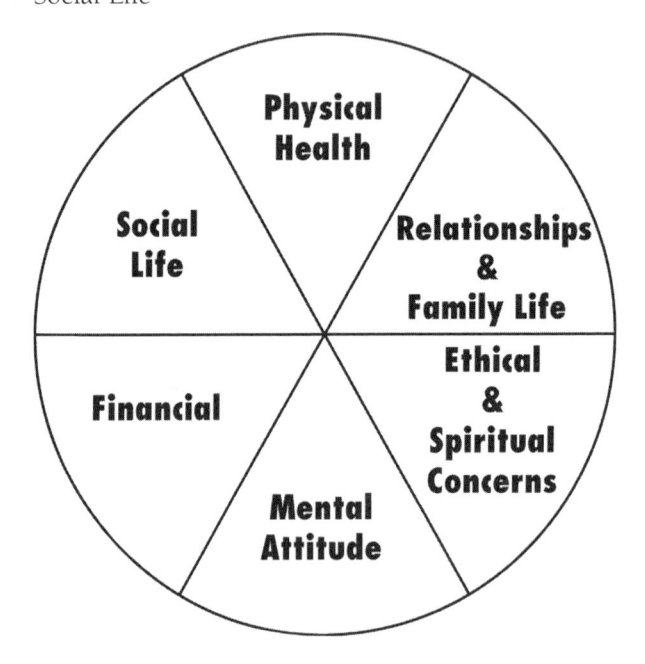

(Wheel of Life diagram with six segments: Physical Health, Relationships & Family Life, Ethical & Spiritual Concerns, Mental Attitude, Financial, Social Life)

Each of these areas plays a role in – and is affected by – all of the stages of a human being's life. Using the next exercise, look at some questions you can ask yourself.

These inquiries do not have to wait until you're at the culmination of your career to be answered. Too many people sacrifice their physical health, their family relationships, and many other of these components while on their way to the top. Although the questions are listed in this book on selling your business, they can be asked at any time in your life.

Your Wheel of Life works just like one of the tires on your car. If it's not periodically checked for air, it can go flat. If there is a weak spot in a tire, a bubble can develop, resulting in a bumpy ride or even a blowout. A misaligned or poorly balanced tire will cause uneven wear and shorten the tire's life. On the other hand, a well-balanced tire that has the right amount of air produces a smooth and comfortable ride.

Here's the Wheel of Life exercise:

First, examine the headings of all six elements.

Second, focus on one area at a time by reading all of the questions related to it.

Next, using a scale of 1 to 10 (1 being low, 5 average, 10 high), for each area, rate your feelings of satisfaction, achievement, delight, or positive fulfillment.

Then, when you've examined all areas, decide which – if any – you wish to improve upon.

Finally, develop a personal action plan for improvement – and begin to put that plan into action.

Physical Health

1. Is physical health important to me?
2. Is my energy level sufficient to do what I'm doing right now?
3. Are my personal habits conducive to good health? Do I get adequate rest and relaxation?
4. Is my body weight conducive to good health?
5. Do I get sufficient exercise?
6. Do I know the danger signs of major diseases?

Rating: 1   2   3   4   5   6   7   8   9   10

Relationships and Family Life

1. Is family life important to me?
2. Do I have specific plans to improve my family life?
3. Do my children or grandchildren like to be with me?
4. Do I give my children or grandchildren, and my mate or significant other, the attention that they deserve?
5. Do I plan regular family activities? Should I?

Rating: 1   2   3   4   5   6   7   8   9   10

Ethical and Spiritual Concerns

1. What are my ethical standards?
2. Is my behavior consistent with those standards?
3. Do I accept full responsibility for my conduct?
4. Do I contribute to religious institutions or other charitable organizations?
5. Do I feel a moral obligation to use my talents and abilities beyond the world of business?
6. Do I recognize the presence of a higher power in my life?

Rating: 1   2   3   4   5   6   7   8   9   10

Mental Attitude

1. Do I strive for self-improvement and development of my full potential?
2. Do I control my own thoughts and emotions?
3. Do I maintain a positive attitude?
4. Do I subscribe to worthwhile magazines and publications?

5. Am I adept at seeing relationships between current events and their ultimate effect on my life?

Rating: 1   2   3   4   5   6   7   8   9   10

Financial

1. How important do I feel money is in my life?
2. Does my income allow me to live in a manner to which I have become accustomed?
3. Do I need to learn more about the world of investments?
4. How good am I at maintaining a personal budget?
5. Do I regularly prepare a written personal financial statement?
6. Do I have adequate health and life insurance?
7. Is there room for financial growth in my life?

Rating: 1   2   3   4   5   6   7   8   9   10

Social Life

1. In general, do I like people?
2. Do I make friends easily?
3. Do I relate well with different kinds of people?
4. Do I have several circles of friends?
5. Am I actively involved in organizations to which I belong?
6. Do I plan my social activities?

Rating: 1   2   3   4   5   6   7   8   9   10

Has this exercise awakened within you any dreams, hopes, or plans that may have been interrupted by your career as a business owner? If so, now might be the time to plan to take action on those aspirations!

The same traits that brought you to successful entrepreneurship – the will to succeed, the creativity, the resourcefulness, and the willingness to risk – will take you wherever you want to go in your life from this point forward.

CHAPTER EIGHT

In Conclusion

In Conclusion

Go back to the beginning

At the beginning of this book, you were asked to think about WHY you are selling.

Maybe it's now time to revisit your answer. Think about the real reasons and make certain that you are not just reacting to a temporary problem or feeling. And, furthermore, that you will be happy with the solution you've chosen.

Common mistakes made by business owners selling their business are these:

1. They decide to sell the business too soon. They may react to a financial climate without really thinking about the non-financial, psychological benefits of being a business owner. These include being in charge, having a place to go every morning, knowing your place in the community.
2. They hold onto the business for too long. In this case, the business may fail because of the owner's physical or emotional inability to run it successfully.
3. They waver. Owners who play with the idea of selling, then go back and forth about their decisions, will lose the momentum and enthusiasm they have used to maintain and increase business.

Perspective of contributing writers...

WHY EXIT PLANNING?

By Kerney Laday Jr. and Doug Ortega

Many owners of privately held businesses have common challenges:
- Owners of closely held and family owned businesses would like to exit the business within the next five years and have no strategy to maximize the value of their business.
- Owners have not taken active steps to transition out of ownership.
- Owners have simply been too busy working in their business to be working on it.

Proper knowledge and preparation can mean millions of dollars to you when you ultimately leave your company. Start Exit Planning today and you can help to avoid the sad (but too common) fate of many business owners.

An Exit Planning process begins by asking yourself the questions that follow. Your Exit Plan will begin to develop as you answer each of the following questions affirmatively:

1. Do you know your retirement goals and what it will take – in cash – to reach them?
2. Do you know how much your business is worth today, in cash?
3. Do you know the best way to increase the income stream generated by your ownership interest?

In Conclusion

4. Do you know how to sell your business to a third party and possibly lower your taxes?
5. Do you know how to transfer your business to family members, co-owners, or employees while lowering taxes and potentially enjoying financial gain?
6. Do you have a continuity plan for your business if the unexpected happens to you?
7. Do you have a plan to help secure finances for your family if the unexpected happens to you?

These questions are almost misleadingly simple to ask, but to answer them affirmatively requires thought and action on your part.

Creating and implementing your Exit Plan may be the most important business and financial event of your life.

Courtesy of Kerney Laday Jr. and Doug Ortega, Managing Partners, Allegiance Business Advisors (ABA), exit planning division of Allegiance Capital Corporation
5429 LBJ Freeway, Suite 750
Dallas, TX 75240
Kerney phone: 214-217-7758
E-mail: kladay@allcapcorp.com
Doug phone: 214-217-7755
E-mail: dorteca@allcapcorp.com
Web: http://www.allcapcorp.com/

Perspective of a contributing writer...

YOU TOO WILL DIE. NOT IF, BUT WHEN
By David Mahmood

Planning for one's death is a topic many people do not like to address. It is one they defer. Sometimes they wait too long. Business owners often drive their company forward with foresight and proactive planning but, surprisingly enough, they frequently fail to plan for the inevitable: death.

Without proper succession and business planning, the unexpected death of a business owner can leave the fate of the company in a precarious state.

- If something happens to you today, who will run the company tomorrow?
- How much will your estate taxes be and have you appropriated sufficient funds?
- If your shares are willed to your spouse or children, are they willing to stay on and run the company or do they prefer liquidity?
- Will a partner take the reins of the company, or will your heirs step in to run the business?
- If you have a partner, will his or her interests conflict with that of your heirs?

These questions, and many others, deserve careful thought and consideration.

Ultimately, you should have a well-defined succession plan in place that you share with family members, partners, and possibly key employees.

For many business owners, the best plan is one in which they sell their business and agree to stay on and run it for a set number of years. This allows them to take a significant amount of cash off the table, meet the needs of their estate, and protect their family and their personal retirement. By selling the business early and agreeing to stay on and work for at least another five years, they put their exit strategy in place and while they are alive, well, and healthy, they can make sound business decisions.

The sale of a business in today's market can easily take nine to 12 months. Agreeing to work another five years means you need to plan a minimum of at least six years in advance before you even consider full or partial retirement. The type of sale where the selling shareholder agrees to stay on and drive the company forward can be done with the owner retaining a piece of equity. This equity hold can be as significant as the seller wishes. At the end of five years, it provides in effect a second sale.

If you have grown the business with the new buyers, you have eliminated the risk of investing the capital, but you enjoy the rewards of the equity you keep being worth significantly more. This type of plan provides you with significant cash at the sale of the company, future employment where you continue to drive the business forward with other people's money; and you get significantly rewarded when you sell the last piece of your equity.

People who plan are generally more successful than those who don't. Waiting 'til the last minute to sell your business is not a plan; it is an act of desperation.

Courtesy of David Mahmood, Founder and
Chairman, Allegiance Capital Corporation
5429 LBJ Freeway, Suite 750
Dallas, TX 75240
Phone: 214-217-7732
E-mail: dmahmood@allcapcorp.com
Web: http://www.allcapcorp.com/

Your worst enemy

You must realize that the greatest obstacle you face in selling your business isn't the leaking roof or the falling profits. It's you. Well, not actually you, but your emotional attachment to the business. The difficulty in cutting the ties with something that you have grown and loved is the main reason you may experience trouble selling – even if everything and everyone tells you that the time is right.

Ultimately, it's you who makes the final choice.

Good luck – and best wishes on the sale of your company!

CHAPTER NINE

Glossary of Terminology

Glossary of Terminology

If you're a "first-timer" to mergers and acquisitions, you'll be encountering terminology that may sound to you like words of a foreign language. Some of the common words used in the deal-making process are explained here.

Acquisition. The process by which the stock or assets of one corporation come to be owned by another entity. The transaction may take the form of a purchase of stock, a purchase of assets, an assumption of liabilities, a reorganization, or a merger.

Add-backs. Any items on a recast financial statement that increase the bottom line profits. In most cases, add-backs will reflect increased profitability that, in turn, makes a company more valuable, especially if it is priced on a "multiple-of-earnings" basis.

Book Value. The accounting of the excess – or deficit – of assets over total liabilities. Net worth, as recorded on a company's balance sheet.

Broker or Business Broker (also see Intermediary). A person who acts for either the buyer or the seller in arranging a transaction of businesses with annual sales of less than one million dollars. Such an individual is involved in searching for appropriate buyers or sellers, and negotiating and structuring the deal. A business broker acts as a financial consultant and advisor to his client.

Capital Gains. Profits from the sale of capital assets. The gain for tax purposes is based on the gross consideration received, less the original basis (cost or price) of the ownership.

Cash Flow. The excess of all cash sources, minus all cash uses. Often defined as a company's cash profit, plus all non-cash expenses.

Closing. The finalization of a transaction, when the conditions of a change of ownership are fulfilled and the funds are transferred.

Consolidation (or "Consolidation Effort" or "Roll-up"). The process of combining a quantity of smaller companies into one larger enterprise for purposes of attaining economies of scale.

Covenant Not to Compete. A section found in most purchase agreements whereby the seller agrees not to compete with the business being sold. To enforce non-compete clauses, courts have deemed that they be specific in activity, place, and time. Buyers often seek to allocate a portion of the purchase price to a "covenant not to compete," especially when they are paying more than the net worth of a company's assets.

Covenant. A clause in a contract concerning acts that a person or organization will or will not perform.

Deal Lawyer (or "Business Transaction Lawyer"). An attorney whose practice specialty is corporate mergers and acquisitions.

Deal Maker. See Intermediary.

Due Diligence. A thorough examination by the buyer to confirm that information provided by the seller is true, complete, and accurate. It also refers to an audit of the seller's financial statements and examination into business records (corporate minutes book) and legal records. The period of "due diligence" usually occurs after a "Letter of Intent" has been signed, but before closing.

Earn-out. Additional payments made to sellers contingent upon their meeting certain performance criteria in the future. Earn-out payments are usually based on meeting certain sales or profitability projections.

EBIT. Earnings before interest and taxes.

Escrow. A "holdback" of a portion of the purchase price pending the attainment of certain conditions. In acquisition matters, buyers may demand that a portion of the purchase price be held in an escrow account for a period of time, pending the outcome of a contingent action, such as collection of accounts receivable.

Fair Market Value. The price that a commodity can bring in an open exchange between buyers and sellers in a free market, when neither the buyer nor the seller is under a time constraint.

Finder. A person who introduces a buyer to a seller, or a seller to a buyer, for a fee. A finder is not an agent for either party. A finder's role is merely to introduce.

Fragmented Industry. A trade, profession, or industry composed of a smattering of mostly smaller companies or businesses, each operating independently. Examples would be plumbing companies, dental practices, automobile towing services, etc.

Goodwill. An intangible asset, representing the excess of the cost of assets over their listed value or market value. Goodwill is usually created by buying assets at a value higher than their fair market value. Goodwill is essentially nothing, because it represents nothing tangible. It is only the perceived value of an acquired company's name, reputation, and anticipated stream of earnings.

Holdback. See Escrow.

Intermediary ("Facilitator," sometimes called "Broker," or "Investment Banker"). A person who acts for either the buyer or the seller in arranging a transaction of businesses with annual sales in excess of one million dollars. Such an individual is involved in searching for appropriate merger candidates, and negotiating and structuring the deal. An intermediary acts as a financial consultant and advisor to his client.

Letter of Intent. A nonbinding, written summary of the buyer's and seller's mutual understanding of the price, terms, and conditions of an acquisition in the process of being negotiated.

Merger. A combining of two businesses into one. In a merger, Company A combines with and disappears into Company B, or creates Company C.

"No-Shop" Clause. An agreement, usually in a Letter of Intent or Purchase Agreement, restricting the seller from either soliciting or engaging in discussions with other potential buyers for a specific period of time (usually 60 to 90 days).

Payback Period. The time required by a buyer to recoup his original investment in a company through its earnings (profits). Generally, buyers expect payback periods of five to seven years, taking into account the time value of money.

Pooling of Interests. An accounting method used in a merger in which the balance sheets of two companies are combined. No goodwill is taken on the surviving company's balance sheet, under the premise that no purchase ever occurred.

Principal. The primary investor in an acquisition. One who will hold most of the equity in the acquired company going forward. A principal is distinguished from an agent or intermediary, who represents one side in a transaction for a fee.

Private Company (or Privately Held Company). A company whose stock is not publicly traded on a stock exchange.

Private Equity Group. A private investment firm focusing on acquiring businesses.

Public Company (or Publicly Held Company). A company whose stock is traded on a stock exchange and whose stock trading and other activities are governed by laws administered by the Securities and Exchange Commission (the SEC).

Purchase Agreement. A legally binding contract for the sale of the stock or assets of a company.

Recasting (of Financial Statements). Revising financial statements to reflect a more accurate picture of the profits of a business.

Representations and Warranties. Binding claims by either party to a transaction. Both buyers and sellers usually warrant certain claims to each other: buyers that they are financially qualified to make the acquisition, and sellers as to the nature and condition of the company being sold.

Seller's Note. A note held by a seller to help finance the purchase of a business. Usually seller's notes are unsecured obligations, though they may be secured by a lien of the assets or the stock of the company.

Synergy. The creation of greater value by combining two or more companies. This may be accomplished through a combination of production or marketing or management skills, or merely a reduction of overhead and an elimination of duplication.

Target Company. A company that his been chosen by a potential buyer as an attractive acquisition candidate.

Terms. Details of an agreement such as price, payment schedule, interest rate, due date, and other various conditions involved in the sale or purchase of a business.

CHAPTER TEN

Internet Resources and Words of Caution!

Internet Resources and Words of Caution!

Internet surfing will reveal many sources of services for business sellers, most claiming that they can "do the job."

Of course, offering your company for sale on the Internet is somewhat akin to "For Sale By Owner" – a move that's highly suspect and questionable. You learned about the pitfalls in Chapter 2.

Your company may be the single biggest asset that you own. Selling it may be the most important financial decision of your entire life. The biggest. It's not something you want to go about impulsively.

Quite frankly, rather than posting your business for sale on the Internet, you may be better served by engaging "face-to-face, boots-on-the-ground" professionals with whom you can interact… in person. That's my advice. You decide!

Of course, online business-for-sale websites can be used as an educational tool. Many of the sites aggregate "business for sale" listings posted by a variety of professionals representing sellers throughout the country. Such sites serve a purpose similar to that of a local residential real estate Multiple Listing Service (MLS), where buyers can visit one website to see all properties for sale in a defined geographic area.

Browsing business for sale websites can provide you with comparative data in relation to your company. These sites often list companies by size of annual sales, cash flow (profitability), and asking price. Though there is no substitute for a professional, in-depth valuation of your business, comparative information can serve as a very general guideline as to the "competition" your selling professional will encounter when placing your company on the market.

Listed below are some online resources. They are ranked in order of popularity by http://alexa.com/ on the day this research was conducted. Alexa is a recognized web information company that provides site ranking services. It computes Internet traffic rankings by synthesizing the web searches of millions of users. (Please note: None of the sites that appear are endorsed by the author. They are simply intended as a "learning tool" for the reader.)

http://www.businessesforsale.com/
Searchable global directory of businesses for sale and brokers.

http://bizbuysell.com/
Listings of business opportunities and resources to assist with buying and selling. In alliance with The Wall Street Journal Online.

http://www.bizquest.com/
Business for sale listings, franchises, and related resources. In alliance with Entrepreneur.com

http://businessbroker.net/
Searchable database of businesses for sale.

http://www.businessmart.com/

Business Mart is a search engine for businesses for sale, finding a business broker in your area, or finding the right franchise. It has small businesses for sale as well as large businesses.

http://www.globalbx.com/

Free business for sale listings, franchise opportunities, commercial loans, and related resources.

http://www.mergernetwork.com/

Matching qualified buyers with quality businesses since 1995.

CHAPTER ELEVEN

Profiles of
Contributing
Writers

Profiles of Contributing Writers

KERNEY LADAY JR.
Managing Partner
Allegiance Business Advisors (ABA)
Exit Planning Division of Allegiance Capital Corporation
5429 LBJ Freeway, Suite 750
Dallas, TX 75240

Direct: 214-217-7758
Fax: 214-217-7780
E-mail: kladay@allcapcorp.com
Web: http://www.allcapcorp.com/

Key achievements:

- More than 20 years experience in sales and marketing with private, public, and government establishments.
- Former owner of multiple companies, with personal experience in starting and selling businesses.
- Demonstrated ability to work with principals of closely held private companies to achieve their goals of selling their company expeditiously, confidentially, and at a premium price.

Kerney provides 20 years of sales and marketing experience with private, public, and government entities. He has specialized in vertical markets such as legal, medical, manufacturing, high technology, engineering, and consumer goods. Kerney began his career with Xerox Corp. and has been trained at Xerox University in Buyer Focus Consultative Selling. In addition, as president and CEO, Kerney founded and built a multimillion-dollar high-technology enterprise that was successfully sold to strategic buyers.

Kerney holds a bachelor's degree in business administration from Nazareth College of Rochester, N.Y. He has lived in France, Germany, New York, Georgia, Louisiana, and Florida. He currently lives in Dallas with his wife and three daughters. He is involved with civic and professional activities and enjoys golf, tennis, cycling, traveling, and reading in his leisure time.

DAVID MAHMOOD
Founder and Chairman
Allegiance Capital Corporation
5429 LBJ Freeway, Suite 750,
Dallas, TX 75240

Direct: 214-217-7732
Fax: 214-217-7751
E-mail: dmahmood@allcapcorp.com
Web: http://www.allcapcorp.com/

Key achievements:

- Corporate executive and entrepreneur who founded, financed, and built eight companies.
- Deal structure specialist with success qualifying and marketing the value of a company to interested buyers or investors.
- Strong negotiator with powerful closing skills.

Over the last decade, David has served as an investment banker managing hundreds of complex, multimillion-dollar transactions in North and South America. His years of experience, ranging from Fortune 500 companies to entrepreneurial startups, gives him firsthand knowledge of a wide variety of business transactions. His ability to create and engineer financial transactions has provided Allegiance with a strong following, including both business owners and shareholders.

David launched his career in Minneapolis and St. Paul, Minn., where he was born and worked for a variety of Fortune 500 companies. His early business career included:

- Earning the distinction as the first licensee for National Football League and American Football League posters.

- Serving as vice president and director of sales for Brown & Bigelow, at the time the world's largest specialty advertising company.
- Working as vice president and director of marketing for CPS Industries, an international consumer products company.
- Creating and developing the Hoyle Playing Card Company by age 28.

Later in his business career, David founded and developed seven companies. He has served on numerous boards and industrial groups. He has been a frequent keynote speaker for national and international trade organizations and universities, and has been featured in numerous publications.

SCOTT D. MASHUDA, CBI (Certified Business Intermediary)
Managing Director
River's Edge Alliance Group, LLC
P.O. Box 24553
Pittsburgh, PA 15234

Phone: 412-894-3244
Fax: 412-592-0929
E-mail: smashuda@RiversEdgeAlliance.com
Web: http://www.riversedgealliance.com/

Scott D. Mashuda has approximately 10 years of mergers and acquisitions, business valuation, and business brokerage experience. He has represented both public and private companies in matters of sale, purchase, valuation, and restructuring.

Before co-founding River's Edge Alliance Group, LLC, Scott worked at the Big 4 accounting firm Ernst & Young as an expert in business valuations.

Industry Experience:

Scott has valued, sold, and/or assisted in the acquisitions of small, closely held businesses in the following industries:

- Distribution
- Manufacturing
- Professional Service Firms (Financial Services / Insurance / Law)
- Hospitality (Bars / Restaurants / Night Clubs)
- Various Retail
- Information Technology
- Medical Device Companies
- Family Entertainment Centers
- Assisted Living Facilities
- Pharmaceutical Companies
- Small Business Machines and POS Systems Companies

- Long-Haul Trucking
- Health & Fitness Centers
- Truck & Automotive Dealerships
- Environmental Consulting
- Plumbing Supply
- Outdoor Advertising
- Automotive Repair / Service
- Chemical Coatings
- Commercial Printing Companies
- Funeral Homes
- Construction / Renovation & Repair

Certifications:
- Certified Business Intermediary (CBI) – International Business Brokers Association
- Licensed Real Estate Salesperson – Commonwealth of Pennsylvania

Education:
Bachelor of Science in Accountancy
Case Western Reserve University, Cleveland, OH

DOUG ORTEGA
Managing Partner
Allegiance Business Advisors (ABA)
Exit Planning Division of Allegiance Capital Corporation
5429 LBJ Freeway, Suite 750
Dallas, TX 75240

Direct: 214-217-7755
Fax: 214-217-7782
E-mail: dortega@allcapcorp.com
Web: http://www.allcapcorp.com/

Key achievements:

Doug is a seasoned executive with more than 20 years of diversified functional and industry experience in both Fortune 500 and startup companies.

- More than 12 years of experience starting, building, and leading high-growth companies in competitive markets.
- Successfully positioned technology company to raise $60 million from multiple-tier 1 VC firms.
- Hands-on experience as a business owner and operator.

Highlights of Doug's career include co-founding an IT professional services firm in 1997 that grew to $135 million in sales in just over seven years. Doug served as president and was responsible for architecting the strategy and managing the growth and global expansion during that period.

Most recently, Doug held the position of Chief Operating Officer of the world's largest aggregator of mobile content for smart phones, where he led worldwide business development, technology, marketing, and customer care.

Earlier in his career, he led the human resource functions for companies in telecommunications outsourcing, and the wholesale distribution business.

Doug has served on the boards of industry trade groups and has been a speaker at national events for the staffing services and the mobile industries.

He attended SMU, where he studied marketing and organizational behavior.

ANDREW ROGERSON, CBI (Certified Business Intermediary)

Owner, Sacramento Office
Murphy Business and Financial Corporation – N CA
777 Campus Commons Road, Suite 200
Sacramento, CA 95825

Phone: 916-570-2674
Fax: 916-644-6330
E-mail: a.rogerson@murphybusiness.com
Web: http://www.andrew-rogerson.com/homepage.htm

Andrew currently holds the Certified Business Intermediary (CBI) designation from the International Business Brokers Association, the highest designation awarded by the IBBA. Andrew has also earned the Certified Business Broker (CBB) designation from the California Association of Business Brokers and the Certified Machinery and Equipment designation (CMEA) from the National Business and Builders Institute.

Murphy Business and Financial Corporation – N CA – is part of one of the largest and most successful national businesses specializing in business valuations, business sales, franchise opportunities, commercial real estate, and equipment appraisals with offices located throughout the United States.

The local office in Sacramento is owned and operated by Andrew Rogerson, with additional offices in Folsom and Davis.

Andrew is a member of the following professional organizations:
- California Association of Business Brokers
- International Business Brokers Association
- Institute of Business Appraisers (past member)
- National Equipment and Business Builders Institute
- Society of Business Analysts
- The Sacramento Metro Chamber of Commerce

GEORGE SIERCHIO

Accredited Business Coach, Seasoned Buy/Sell Intermediary, Speaker and Author
Action Business Partners, Inc.
PO Box 5454
Parsippany, NJ 07054

Phone: 973-394-9800
Fax: 1-866-321-1454
E-mail: info@actionbusinesspartners.com
Web: http://actionbusinesspartners.com/

George Sierchio is a degreed electrical engineer who has never worked full time for anyone but himself. In the last 16-plus years, he has owned and operated several businesses in a variety of fields including engineering/IT consulting, design services, online retail, and bar/restaurants.

Within these businesses, he has started five from scratch, bought one, and sold two. This includes a business that he brought to the million-dollar mark in just four years' time more than 10 years ago. He's helped start several businesses for clients, worked to acquire client funding, and has assisted many entrepreneurs to buy and sell businesses as an advisor as well as an intermediary.

Since 2003, he has advised hundreds of entrepreneurs through his articles, blog contributions, books, seminars, and coaching programs. All of these business owners have used George's experience and "new school" style of applying the best processes, procedures, and systems from a variety of industries to achieve their business and personal goals in half the time it would take to do it themselves.

George has been sought out to participate in events and contribute articles to numerous technology business owner organizations and associations, as well as not-for-profit business incubators. He has also been invited several times as a guest lecturer at Rutgers University, Seton Hall, and Fairleigh Dickinson University for entrepreneurship, business finance and negotiations courses.

With his extensive successful entrepreneurial experience and technical background, George continues to inspire, encourage, and push technical business owners to achieve the highest goals. He uses a unique style to squeeze the most productivity and money out of businesses by teaching owners the best techniques in time management, leadership, financial metrics, client management, marketing, employee management, and building business value for exit strategies.

George is also the author of two books:

B.Y.O.B - Build Your Own Business, Don't Be Your Own Boss, a must-read book for those looking to operate a successful consulting or service business.

B.Y.O.B - Buy Your Own Business, an e-book education and reference book that's part of his Buy Your Own Business Toolkit.

ERIC R. VOTH
Principal
ERV Productions, Inc.
19102 Polo Meadow Drive
Humble, TX 77346

Desk: 281-852-4707
E-mail: eric@ervproductions.com
Web: http://ervproductions.com/

Eric R. Voth is a serial entrepreneur... a producer, consultant, author, and publisher.

During the course of his career, Eric has personally undertaken...

- The start-up of 10 independent businesses.
- The purchase of five independent businesses.
- The sale of five independent companies (two of which were actually mergers).
- The start-up of four franchisee operations.
- The loss of investment in four independent ventures that were unsuccessful.

As a producer, Eric creates concepts for television shows and pitches them for consideration to cable and broadcast networks.

As a Business Transaction Consultant, Eric is not Business Broker. Rather, he primarily functions as a "matchmaker" by assisting business owners with the selection of appropriate, qualified, professionals to serve as advocates in the sale of their firms.

He became involved in the business transaction field after merging his own company in 1993. Eric is former Board

Chairman of Akron, Ohio, based Physicians & Surgeons (P&S) Ambulance Service. He and his business partner bought the business in 1972, with no money down. In 1994, during an industry-wide consolidation — in a pooling of interest transaction — they merged their company with American Medical Response Inc. (EMT), the first ambulance service to be publicly-traded on the New York Stock Exchange.

From 1981 through 1992, while chairman of his own firm, Eric was also a professional speaker. He specialized in presenting topics on small business management — mostly to company owners — at conventions, conferences and meetings throughout the United States, sponsored by trade and professional associations.

Eric and his business partner, Ron Myers, co-authored a book entitled THE NEW OWNER: MAKING THE TRANSITION FROM EMPLOYEE TO EMPLOYER, released by publisher Business One Irwin in March, 1993. The book is designed to serve as an instruction manual and is targeted toward two audiences. The first is current business owners who want a blueprint by which to more effectively manage their companies. The second audience is employees of small businesses who aspire someday to become company owners.

He is author and publisher of the book, HOW TO SELL YOUR PRIVATELY OWNED COMPANY — A BASIC GUIDE FOR INDEPENDENT BUSINESS OWNERS — BABY BOOMER'S EDITION.

Eric credits much of his success to the application of ideas he learned from others. He synthesized information from numerous sources, then adapted and applied it in his own life. He helped build his companies using principles from books such as THINK AND GROW RICH by Napoleon Hill, THE MAGIC OF BELIEVING, by Claude Bristol, WHAT TO SAY

WHEN YOU TALK TO YOUR SELF, by Dr. Shad Helmstetter, and the *ADVENTURES IN ATTITUDES* course by Bob Conklin.

In 1995, Eric relocated from the Akron, Ohio, area to Houston, Texas. He regularly spends time in both locales.

—The End—